Previous Bo

The Work We Were Born To Do

Unconditional Success

Powerful Beyond Measure

The 12 Principles of The Work We Were Born To Do

How to Be Inspired

Over the past two decades, Nick Williams has travelled the world sharing a life-affirming – and profoundly spiritual – vision of work and entrepreneurship. A sought-after international speaker, author and broadcaster, Nick is on a mission to help people move beyond their fears, play a bigger part in their lives, and turn their passions into profitable businesses.

Nick left a deeply unfulfilling (yet outwardly successful) career in IT sales to build his own successful business and – having inspired tens of thousands of people to discover the work they were born to do – he's one of the few personal development experts who truly walks-the-talk.

A former trustee of Alternatives at St James's (a premier venue in London for major authors and workshop leaders from around the world), Nick is also the co-founder of The Inspired Entrepreneurs Club: the world's only learning community and free social network for Inspired Entrepreneurs. He has been widely featured in the media as a leading authority on the world of work and on how our work can be an expression of the very best of us.

Dedication

I dedicated this book to all those awakened and
awakening souls whose work is their love made visible.
Thank you

To Aiste
Be inspired!
[signature] I love
Nick

The Business You Were Born To Create

How to make your living doing
the work you were born for

A handbook for
Inspired Entrepreneurs

Nick Williams

Balloonview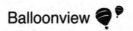

Balloon View Ltd
Brensett Place
Brenzett, Kent
TN29 0ET
www.balloonview.com

Cover photo by Sharron Wallace

ISBN 978-1-907798-07-8

Printed in the United Kingdom for Balloon View Ltd by
CPI Bookmarque Ltd, Croydon, CR0 4TD

A CIP Catalogue record for this book is available from the British Library.

www.balloonview.com

Contents

Acknowledgements

Thanks to Helen Bee for our fourteen years of love, encouragement and friendship. To my mum, Pam, for her continued love and support, and to the memory of my father, Harold, and his enduring love. To my sister Amanda. To Niki Hignett for friendship, his brilliance and our constant re-invention, and Ali for generously loaning him to our business.

To all our speakers at Inspired Entrepreneur for your generosity and desire to contribute, and to all the volunteers at the evenings: Susie, Angela, Wendy, Jo and Chris.

To Rick Arrandale for his legacy to me, mentoring me and his continuing contribution to our thinking, even though he died in 2008.

To Julia McCutchen for friendship, our work together and publishing me in the first place. To Judy Piatkus for coffee and friendship. To Peter Carey for friendship and helping me face my guilt about playing pool during the day.

To Sue Lascelles for fabulous editing skills.

Mil and Ralph for being great neighbours and for welcoming me into their family. Thanks to their children Hilary and Carolyn too.

To Adam Stern, Matt Ingrams and Martin Wenner for eighteen years of friendship – and counting.

To 'The Group' – Juliette, Peter, Jan and Linda and Catherine, whom we lost to cancer so sadly in July 2010.

To our Friday night family – Ros, Barry, Louise and Rita, and also to Martin and Amanda, Steven, Hayley and Ava Grace, and finally Eddie, Rafe, Zach, Dawn, Annette, Carly and Susan.

To Dipak for being an inspiration and all at the Saturday morning yoga group

To the MKP I-Group and all their support, and the MKP Elders Group too.

Rick and Helen for precious friendship.

To Dr Robert Holden, as ever, for friendship and being a travelling companion.

To Charlie Jordan for your friendship and being the greatest foodie I know, and for introducing me to Ottolenghis.

To Kurt April for the opportunity to come down to South Africa again and for being my advocate. To Kate Emmerson and Stripey for lovely times in Johannesburg.

To Ed Peppitt – you are a real find!

To Zerah and all our friends at the Pia Bella in Kyrenia and to John and Elaine in Bellapais.

Chris and Sylvina for friendship, and to Howard and Trish for friendship.

Mark Shaw for friendship and 'Nick and Mark do latte in Finchley'.

Alicia, for helping my entrée into the world of VAs be fairly painless and easy.

To Michael Daly, my Irish soul brother, for walks in Malahide and celebrating each other's growth.

For all my years of involvement at Alternatives and the gifts I got from being there. I was sorry to have to leave.

To Alex Armitage for his gracious invitations to apple picking in Great Offley and for being one of the best hosts I have ever met.

To Jeff Allen – soul brother whose love and insight always save my ass when I hit rock bottom, and for being a good friend, and to Chuck and Lency Spezzano for continuing inspiration.

And always to *A Course in Miracles*, for being the beacon of light on my way home.

Introduction

I have always been fascinated by the idea of potential, of that which lies invisible within us, but which might one day become seen and known in the outside world. I am intrigued by questions such as: 'How many sunflowers are there in potential in a head of sunflower seeds?' The answer is, of course, limitless. The same applies to our potential as human beings. There is so much in potential in all of us. The word 'potential' comes from the Latin potentialis, meaning 'that which is possible' and potentia – 'power'. Sadly, when we are growing up most of us aren't told, 'You are an incredible being with amazing potential. Your life can be a journey into discovering and revealing that potential.' Instead, we are told that we have to work and get a job, even if we don't enjoy it – that's just how life is. More often than not, we are told what isn't possible for us.

When I was young, I always felt that I had a lot of potential. But I squashed down that yearning in order to fit in, get a job and career, and to be 'normal'. By my late twenties normal was killing me, if not quite literally then certainly emotionally and spiritually. I longed for the freedom to do my own thing, to be in charge of my own life, to make a difference, to have a life that was inspiring and which had meaning to it – and which contributed to the world beyond myself.

The yearning to fulfil my true potential eventually led me to find the courage to quit my corporate job and start my own business. I wasn't – and still am not – that interested in business per se. However, I am deeply interested in people and their potential, and in how to realise that potential so we can all lead happy, fulfilled and meaningful lives. And I have discovered that for many of us the experience of running our own business, doing work we love, is one of the most exciting and suitable vehicles for the discovery of and fulfilment of our innate potential. You too may suspect there are potential books, programmes, businesses, talents and gifts in you. And there are! But it is up to you to make that potential real in this world.

That's why I co-founded the Inspired Entrepreneurs Community (see page 191), which I love – at its core, it's simply a vehicle to help people become happy by fulfilling their potential and bringing whatever is inside them out into this world. If you decide to join us, you will have the chance to give birth to that which exists in embryo in you right now. Far from being self-indulgent, achieving your potential is actually a very generous thing for you to do: just think how much richer this world will be when you contribute more of the potential that lies inside you…

We were not designed or destined to be passive and compliant beings; our true nature impels us to be active and engaged. In our hearts, we know that the richest experiences of our lives aren't the result of our yearning for validation, approval or even money. They come when we listen to and act upon our own inner voice, when we are naturally inspired to do something that matters to us, and to do it well – in the service of something greater than ourselves. We are not naturally wired to respond to rewards and punishments, but we are fuelled by a deep-seated desire to direct our own lives, to extend and expand our capabilities, living a life of purpose.

However, the journey towards realising your potential is not for the fainthearted. It can be a joyful and happy path, yet also one strewn with obstacles and challenges. You may have grown up with a work ethic that has constricted your spirit or even disconnected you from your spirit completely. You may have been encouraged to do work that you didn't enjoy so that you would make your parents proud, fit in or just because you believed you had to. Somewhere along the line most of us have been taught to disconnect our hearts and our heads, and so we separate our livelihoods from our souls. Well, it's reconnection time!

Your work shouldn't be a source of suffering, but can indeed be a blessing, a way that you share your unique God-given gifts and talents with the world. Your work, as the poet and philosopher Kahlil Gibran said so beautifully, can be 'love made visible'.

And now, more than ever, the opportunity exists for you to do what you love and to love what you do. But it does mean seeing through new eyes, shedding the years of conditioning you may have grown up with, and glimpsing new possibilities that you didn't even realise existed.

For many of us, the best way to capitalise on these new opportunities is to have our own business, either full time or part time. But most of us will not go into business purely for the sake of it; instead, we simply want the autonomy to be in charge of our lives, to have a meaningful sense of purpose in what we do, and to be free to become good at doing things that mean something to us, whilst earning the money we need to live well.

However, the majority of us may have had no training when it comes to running our own business, because we will have been employed all our lives. When we were growing up, 'Running Your Own Business' was not a career option that was ever suggested to us. So now we have to adopt a new way of looking at the world through creative and entrepreneurial eyes; we need to realise that we can take charge of our own lives and be the initiating force in them. If we do, we will be guided towards discovering the best that is in us and expressing that part of ourselves through our work and business.

Running your own business while doing something that you love, and which is meaningful to you, is very different from running a business mainly to make money. This book is my humble offering to help you map out the terrain of what's involved in running your own business, doing something you love. The Business You Were Born to Create will provide the canvas on which to explore and express the best that is in you. It will show you what it means to follow a deeper sense of personal calling and vocation. To make the difference in the world that you can uniquely make. And to become all that you are capable of being and achieving. Discovering the business you were born to create is such an exciting path, so full of rewards, possibilities, joy and fulfilment, and yet – as we will see – also strewn with obstacles, hazards and challenges that might threaten to make you lose your way.

I hope my twenty years of experience will light up the path you are creating for yourself, and help you reach your potential and the joy that is possible.

Nick Williams, London, October 2010

Section 1:

Being a Pioneer into a Work Ethic of Joy

For hundreds of years, people have lived by a work ethic of struggle, suffering and even misery, believing that work is something that simply has to be endured to provide the income they need in order to enjoy the rest of their lives.

Today, you are called to find your unique vocation and to discover a work ethic of joy. This means work that utilises the best of you, your talents, your gifts and your best spiritual self. Instead of chasing success, follow your joy.

The emerging new work ethic of joy

'People who follow their joy discover a depth of creativity and talent that inspires the world.'

Dr Robert Holden
Author of Be Happy!

For the last two hundred years or so, the dominant work ethic has been something akin to this: don't expect to enjoy your work very much, as work is not to be enjoyed, but endured. Other people create jobs and employment, and we take those jobs because we need the money to survive materially and financially. The more we suffer and sacrifice ourselves in our work, the nobler we become. However, it is possible for us to take responsibility for meeting our obligations in a lighter and more joyful way.

Today, fewer people are willing to tolerate the old dominant work ethic. We know in our hearts that work can be so much more. It can be a meaningful activity, allowing us to share our unique gifts and talents with others and make a positive difference. It can allow us to unwrap our own potential, and be a source of passion and joy, as well as enable us to earn a living. Work can provide structure, meaning, friendship, confidence and self-worth. We are beginning to realise that our work can open the doors to our hearts.

A work ethic of joy and fulfilment is emerging. You may no longer be willing to be a wage slave or a cog in a big machine. You may instead want to inhabit your individuality, live from a sense of purpose, have autonomy and even have the opportunity to become brilliant and masterful at your work. Your work can become the shoreline on which the best of you is made visible in the world. Claude Whitmyer, founder of the Centre for Good Work, puts it this way: 'The real purpose of work is to give us an opportunity to practise being human and to discover everything we are and all that we can be, both as individuals and as members of a community.'

Today, we don't need to choose a particular career path as much as we need to create work and opportunities around what we love doing. In these financially unstable times, sacrificing ourselves in return for a regular income is no longer a safe option. Distorting yourself to fit the mould that you think an employer wants you to inhabit may help you survive in the short term, but this type of behaviour no longer buys security and ultimately it will damage your soul. The new security lies in being your best self, uncovering your unique brilliance and finding the people who need and want your brilliance in their work, business or lives.

Our family, schools, careers advisors and bosses didn't tell us about this emerging world, so this is new territory for most of us. As we haven't been here before, we all are all pioneering together. If this emerging world of work appeals to you, then you are what my friend Christine Livingston calls 'a New Work Pioneer', which she defines as 'feisty, courageous and professional people who are fed up with work as it has been'. Entering it means you are leading in your own life. You are breaking free of your work- and career-conditioning, and forging your own path based on your own values, passions and interests. You aren't just rebelling against work as it has been, but also listening to and heeding a deeper call.

This is exciting but can be scary, and involves maturing and growing up with respect to the attitude we take to work. We need to take responsibility for our work and career as we can no longer rely on employers to take care of us. Even if we are employed, we will need to recognise our own skills and talents, and see ourselves as the suppliers of what we do well.

Your work was born with you

'No one was born into the world whose work is not born with him.'

James Russell Lowell (1891–91)
American poet, essayist, critic and diplomat

Today, the idea of a vocation or calling can seem like a quaint throwback to an earlier age. Personally, I think there has never been a greater need for us to re-engage with the idea of each of us having a calling – what I call 'the Work We Were Born to Do'. I don't think we are born as blank slates waiting for the world to stamp its imprint on us. I do believe we are born as highly individuated souls, with a set of preferred activities and talents – but more than that: with an inexplicable inner knowledge of the things we are meant to do and be, the changes we are meant to make in the world. We are each of us inexorably drawn to particular activities, ideas, issues and causes. As the American philosopher and psychologist Abraham Maslow said, 'A musician must make music, an artist must paint, a poet must write, if he is to be ultimately at peace with himself. What a man can be, he must be.'

So, what is the work that was born with you?

Sadly, most of us weren't encouraged as youngsters to believe in or explore the idea of a personal vocation. Instead, we were most likely encouraged to go against our own grain, to work for survival rather than for joy.

This can cause us great suffering as it means we aren't free to give voice to our own unique song in life or to play our unique part in creation. When we don't hear our true calling, and so fail to enjoy the adventure that life is offering us individually, existence can seem dry and painful. Fully lived lives can serve as a source of inspiration to others, whereas the unhappiness caused by unlived lives can infect those around us – which means that finding and doing the work we love is actually a very generous act.

I have come to believe that each of us has a personal calling that's as individual as our fingerprints, and that the best way for us to succeed in being happy and fulfilled is to discover what we love and then find a way to offer it to others in the form of service – allowing the inspiration of the Universe to lead and guide us. You are here because of the unique gift that only you can give to the world, in your own way. Your vocation is what you are called to fulfil with your life's energy. It will inspire you and perhaps scare you too, but ultimately, through pursuing it, you will discover that your love is greater than your fear and that miracles can happen when you give as much energy to your dreams as you do to your fears.

Naturally inspired to work at what you love

'Many entrepreneurs ask me, "Where is the market opportunity – where can I make lots of money?" I tell them to think this way instead: "What are you so passionate about doing that you'd be happy doing it for ten years, even if you never made a dime? That's the business you should start and be in. Ironically, you will end up making money. So, chase the vision and the higher purpose, not the money."'

Tony Hsieh Zappos
Former CEO of the largest online shoe store, Zappos.com,
with a turnover of over $1 billion

Who said we had to dislike our work? Somewhere in the past, probably around the time of the Industrial Revolution in the eighteenth and nineteenth centuries, there entered into the collective psyche the idea that work was an intrinsically disagreeable activity which we'd rather not be doing. To get people to work, then, required motivating them through the use of rewards or the threat of punishment. People had to be manipulated to work, as left to their own devices they would be lazy and not perform. Even though the appearance of most workplaces has transformed radically in the last two to three hundred years, much of the thinking of the Industrial Age still lives on within them today.

I am not sure that this way of thinking was ever true, but it has certainly become the reality for so much of the world's population. Rewards and punishments have the greatest impact when someone is trying to get us to do something that goes against our grain and which we'd rather not be doing. There is, however, a considerable amount of evidence which shows quite the opposite to be true: that when we are given autonomy, have a meaningful sense of a larger purpose to what we do, and are free to master the talents and skills of our own choice, we are intrinsically motivated to work. This kind of work also puts us in the state of 'flow' described by the American psychologist Mihaly Csikszentmihalyi – a state of enjoyment, creativity and total involvement. We don't need to be rewarded or punished in order to perform; instead, we engage naturally with our work, and when we are intrinsically motivated there is an element of artistry to our work. We perform naturally at our peak.

Economic theory assumes human beings are profit-maximisers, whilst the reality is that we tend to be purpose-maximisers. We crave an inspiring and meaningful purpose more than a new job title. We seek to become what we can become, to be significant and contribute to the greater good. We care about our own needs but also reach beyond ourselves to contribute to the good of others too.

The trend today towards mastery, autonomy and the realisation of a sense of purpose leads us towards creating and running our own businesses, doing work we enjoy and find meaningful. Our businesses can be a canvas for our artistry. We will find that we want to create our own conditions in which we can do our best work, allowing our best nature to come to the surface. Our richest experiences often result from listening to our inner voice, doing something well that matters to us, and doing it in service of a cause greater than ourselves.

You too have an inner drive for autonomy, self-determination, belonging, flourishing into your potential, connecting with others and contributing beyond yourself. When those drives are acknowledged, honoured and liberated, you will achieve more and lead a richer life. You will become better and better at doing something that means something to you. As we often equate the word 'work' with something we don't really want to do, perhaps you will need a new word for the work that you are inspired and willing to do – and which you love to do. There is a willing worker in you.

What is your word for the work you are naturally inspired to do?

Focus on your brilliance and delegate the rest

*'The greatest art is to be oneself. This naturally
follows from living your purpose rather than
living for approval. Otherwise you could end up
in the obituaries under someone else's name. Your
purpose is what you, of all people, can do best. Most
people are frightened of their own purpose, and are
frightened of their own love, passion and happiness.'*

Chuck Spezzano
Author and teacher

Many people believe that running your own business
is about being professional and competent at
everything that needs doing. You become both Chief
Cook and Bottle Washer. But when you are doing what
you love, you need to start thinking differently. Your job
is to focus on what you love and do brilliantly – and then
allow other people to start to do the rest.

Your job is to know that there is a brilliance in you, then
to find and acknowledge that brilliance – honour it,
develop it, hone it, evolve it, show up with it, package
and deliver it to the people who would love to buy it
from you. Then you can start to outsource, delegate, get
help with, barter and exchange the rest of the stuff you
don't like or that you simply aren't that good at. There
are other people who are brilliant at the stuff you are
rubbish at and who will happily do it better than you.

Please don't doubt that there is brilliance in you: it came with your creation and you are on this planet to share your brilliance! You may ask for a brilliant business idea, a brilliant business, job or career, but the most powerful prayer of all is: 'Dear God, please deliver me to my brilliance so that I may bring it to my work, my clients, my business and career.' You are here to shine a light.

Soon after starting my business in 1990, I voluntarily registered for VAT (Valued Added Tax), so that I would look credible to the companies I worked with. I taught myself how to do my VAT returns every quarter, even though I hated having to do them and dreaded the HM Revenue & Customs envelope landing on my doormat. I was still deeply entrenched in the 'making myself do what I didn't really want to be doing' mindset. If I am honest, I was making myself suffer and being a bit of a martyr. Then one day I spoke to my accountant and I asked if she had a bookkeeper who could do my VAT returns for me. She told me she did, and when I asked how much the service would cost, she said, 'About £50 a quarter, so about £200 a year.' I nearly fell over. Why was I making myself suffer so much when for £200 a year I could free myself up?

I have experienced the same thing when writing books: I have become a better writer by letting someone else edit my work for me. I focus on getting my insights and ideas down onto paper, and then delegate to Sue, whose brilliance is editing. My business partner, Niki, is brilliant at strategy, copywriting and software development, at which I am not so good. Our VA (virtual assistant), Alicia, is brilliant at our administration and project management.

Remember, you are here to shine, not struggle.

One strand of employed thinking is, 'we'll ignore what you are great at and focus on your weaknesses – and look at how you can address them'. This ties in beautifully with the Protestant work ethic of suffering, which says that as long as we are going against our own grain, as long as we are suffering, struggling and unhappy, then this is 'real work' and we deserve to be paid for it.

There are always some things you have to do which you'd rather not be doing, but generally don't try to become good at something that simply isn't a natural fit for you. Focus instead on developing what comes naturally to you and, where possible, delegate the rest so that you can tap freely into your own reservoirs of energy and inspiration, rather than waste precious resources unnecessarily.

It is OK for you not to suffer in your work – to experience joy, to be happy and for it still to be work for which you deserve to be paid. Ditch the guilt! Relinquish the suffering ethic! Very few people will hire you because of what a martyr you are. They'll hire you because your energy is high and you are brilliant at whatever they need help with. As an Inspired Entrepreneur, you job is to keep recognising, listening out for and acknowledging your own brilliance – what you most love doing and what adds most to the people you serve. You also need to begin to distinguish between what actually is your work and the manifestation of your personal brilliance, and what supports your work and your brilliance. Too often we think of everything around us as 'work'.

Let your inspiration lead you to your brilliance

'Most people live in a very restricted circle of their potential being. We all have reservoirs of energy and genius to draw upon of which we do not dream.'

William James (1842–1910)
Psychologist and philosopher

Inspiration is the force that will awaken you to your greatest potential; it is what points you towards and helps you unlock your greatest and highest abilities. Inspiration is smelling salts for the soul. When you are in the presence of inspiration, and when you follow your own sense of inspiration, possibilities will awaken in you; gifts and talents that have lain dormant will come alive.

One of the most beautiful expressions of this process comes from Patanjali, the compiler of the Yoga Sutras, who wrote 2,200 years ago: 'When you are inspired by some great purpose, some extraordinary project, all your thoughts break your bonds: your mind transcends limitations, your consciousness expands in every direction, and you find yourself in a new, great and wonderful world. Dormant forces, faculties and talents become alive, and you discover yourself to be a greater person by far than you ever dreamed yourself to be.' Inspiration is a phenomenon that can guide us to evolve through the whole of our working lives.

There are four key ways to follow and nurture your sense of inspiration in your work and business:

1. Know what your wells of inspiration are; what it is that uplifts and inspires you.

2. Spend time at your wells of inspiration. Invest time, energy and money in keeping your soul aloft.

3. Seek out new wells of inspiration, such as things that make you go, 'Wow, aren't human beings amazing? Isn't life wonderful?' Affirm life.

4. Become a source of inspiration to yourself by acting in the face of your fears and doubts, and before you feel completely confident. Become courageous.

Sadly, in my experience, we are very quick to dismiss our own inspired ideas, thinking that they are just too big, scary or impossible to pursue. We don't recognise that they are an invitation to us to grow and blossom, to see beyond our fears and limiting beliefs to our greater selves.

Re-examine any brilliant ideas that you may have dismissed, but which won't go away. They may actually hold the clues to your joy and your fulfilment in your work. Your ideas have a life of their own and will help you grow, evolve and become so much more than you ever dreamed possible.

Maybe you are a renaissance soul?

'There was a time, of course, when it was assumed that a person could be many different things. During the period known as the Renaissance, when the creative spirit was in full bloom, it was not unusual for an individual to be a poet, business owner, artist, soldier, linguist and lover.'

Barbara Winter
Author of Making a Living without a Job

Most of us grew up believing that a 'proper job' means working for someone else, doing mainly just the one thing and probably not enjoying it very much – but the fact that you are reading this book means that you are probably redefining what a proper job means for you. Today, a proper job can be pretty much anything we want it to be.

Most of the Inspired Entrepreneurs I have met actually don't want to do just the one thing: they have multiple interests, passions and gifts, so they don't want to lead lives in which they have to leave out significant parts of themselves. Instead, they want lives in which all of their gifts are utilised in the best way possible.

It has never been more possible than it is today to create a portfolio life, or to be what I call a 'renaissance soul'. The beauty of being a renaissance soul is that you can potentially create the business and lifestyle that support you perfectly as an individual. You can build your business and work around yourself, your family, your own needs, your talents, your interests and passions.

If the idea of becoming a renaissance soul appeals to you, you may find that, besides the practical obstacles, the biggest block to creating this way of being may be your conditioning, which tells you, 'I shouldn't try to be a Jack-of-all-trades, because if I do then I'll become a master of none – and no one will take me seriously.' And your inner conditioning may also tell you: 'But won't this way of working confuse people as they won't be able to slot me into a convenient box?'

I suspect that your spirit and your intelligence are way too big to fit into any one job or career. I have seen so many people cause themselves so much pain by trying to squeeze their spirit into a job that simply wasn't big enough for them, rather than try to create work which allowed all of themselves to be expressed and utilised.

Parallel to the idea of being a renaissance soul runs the idea of multiple streams of income. Most of us have been brought up to believe that we should concentrate on just one major source of income – usually defined by our job or career; we believe that if we are going to try to do our own thing, we will need to find another new single source of income. But in truth the, say, £40,000 we need to support ourselves might not all come from one single source. We may instead create four different sources of income, which generate £10,000 each. That can be much more do-able, and opens the door to creative thinking and possibility.

Many people are already living as renaissance souls: Emma Jones, founder of Enterprise Nation, estimates that in the UK today, over five million people have part-time businesses which they run alongside their jobs and careers. She calls these people '5 to 9'ers', and their number is growing.

All of us can find ways to be renaissance souls and create extra strands to our core businesses. Your own portfolio may centre on one grand passion, or it may have many seemingly disparate strands and the only commonality is that you love them all – and that you express a different aspect of yourself through each of them.

My health warning would simply be this: don't try to start up too many different activities at once, especially if you are new to an entrepreneurial way of working. By all means design the perfect portfolio lifestyle that inspires and excites you, but acknowledge that it may take you some years to bring everything you want into existence. Sketch out the big picture, but aim to get one or two elements of it filled in first. Some strands of your portfolio will need to generate income immediately, whilst other strands may involve more gradual development so that you can aim to generate income from them in three, six or twelve months' time. So, create some income first, build your confidence, make some mistakes and learn…

Once one or two elements are working well for you, you'll have the knowledge and confidence you need to start focusing on new strands. And you'll be able to apply what you have already learned to deal with the new strands of your work more successfully, becoming a true renaissance soul.

Pioneering with courage

'Courage is the ability to cultivate a relationship with the unknown; to create a form of friendship with what lies around the corner over the horizon – with those things that have not yet come fully into being.'

David Whyte
Poet and author of Midlife and the Great Unknown

To be a pioneer takes courage. By definition, pioneering means going into what is unknown, at least what is unknown by us in our lives so far. In the success story of our lives, we will find ourselves making some brave decisions; we will exhibit true courage when we take action in spite of our fears. In fact, we can *only* really experience courage in the face of fear.

Fear is our greatest obstacle to living happier, more peaceful and powerful lives. One definition of fear is the 'anticipation of pain', but since anticipation necessarily looks towards the future and the future only exists in our imaginations, fear does not exist in reality. Although we can obviously experience fear, it only lives in our minds and in our thoughts.

The good news is that, to create the business we were each born to create, we don't need to have mastered our response to fear already, but we do need to be willing to face our fears and act in spite of them. Deep down, we know that on the other side of each of our fears lies a new slice of freedom. We know that we can be liberated from our fears when we have the courage to face them.

Reaching our innate potential is not so much about doing big things when the feeling hits us; it's more about doing little things every day that move us toward ours dream. It is in fact a daily practice. As psychologist Abraham Maslow said, 'One can choose to go back toward safety or forward toward growth. Growth must be chosen again and again; fear must be overcome again and again.' Reaching our innate potential and pioneering with courage is about staying steady and on course in spite of our fears, large and small.

When you courageously pioneer your way past a fear or challenge, you will help many more people than yourself. So take chances, have the courage to make mistakes if necessary – that's how you will grow. Pain nourishes courage. We sometimes have to fail in order to practise being brave.

Section 2:

Being an Inspired Entrepreneur

Traditional models of entrepreneurship are often based on a person's being driven, competitive, and putting money and ego first – but this doesn't necessarily sit comfortably with us when we are doing work that we intrinsically love. On the contrary, Inspired Entrepreneurs have awakend to their purpose rather than driven by money, and they are always on the look out for great strategies and techniques which can be used in the service of being themselves and doing what they love.

This new entrepreneurial spirit is based on purpose, inspiration, contribution and collaboration. In essence, we can be ourselves and wrap a business around who we are.

A new and inspiring way to be entrepreneurial

'Our bottom line is measured by our character as much as our profits. The joyfully jobless often pursue lines of work that make a difference to the rest of the world, that are more than just a way to earn food to eat and a roof over our heads. We see our business as a natural extension of who we are and what we love to do. We have spent time and energy exploring and understanding ourselves so that we could find ways to earn a living by being ourselves.'

Barbara J. Winter
Author of Making a Living without a Job

What comes to your mind when you think of the word 'entrepreneur'? We all bring our own past experiences, images and examples to the table when we answer that question. For me, the most significant words that used to come to my mind were qualities: I grew up believing that entrepreneurs were greedy, competitive, dodgy, money-driven and ego-maniacs. No prizes for guessing that my role models had included Gordon Gekko from the 1987 film *Wall Street* (whose signature line was 'greed, for lack of a better word, is good'), Arthur Daley in the TV series *Minder* ('have I got a deal for you?'), and Del Boy in the hit TV show *Only Fools and Horses* ('dodgy deals are us').

Until the age of thirty-one, I had always been employed by large companies. As I grew up, 'running your own business' was never once suggested to me as a career choice I might make. But I always felt an entrepreneurial spirit stirring within me, and a call to do my own thing. I cared about people and their potential. I liked being in charge of my life. I craved freedom. I wanted to do something that would make other people's lives better and which I could feel fulfilled doing. I felt I had more potential than my bosses ever wanted from me. And I increasingly hated 'just doing a job'.

But with those guys – Gekko, Daley and Del Boy – as my entrepreneurial role models, you could count me out! I wondered if I was deluding myself when I thought about running a business of my own: I certainly didn't want to be like any of them. Maybe I was mistaken when it came to my own instincts and I didn't really have what it took to be an entrepreneur. So I wondered whether I should become a priest or a social worker instead.

I had no vision or role models that could show me how to be entrepreneurial in the ways that I felt in my heart I could be. I didn't know then that being truly enterprising is about much more than mere entrepreneurship: it is about being an active agent in shaping the future and contributing to the good of others.

Although there are many different ways of being entrepreneurial, Inspired Entrepreneurs are a particular breed who share some common traits:

- They love being in charge of their time and talents, and are motivated to follow their joy and a sense of fulfilment.
- They want to make a good living, but are not purely money-driven.

- They want to make a difference and enrich the lives of their fellow human beings.
- They are curious about their own growth and potential, and are passionate about becoming all that they are capable of becoming.
- They want an inspiring lifestyle, not just a great business.
- They want their lives to be whole and the different elements of their lives to be integrated.
- In essence, they want to be themselves in all areas of their lives.

Basically, being an Inspired Entrepreneur is about building a business around the unique person you already are. It is also a wonderful way to have autonomy over your own life, to make a living, learn and grow, and make a contribution to society.

You can have the love and the money

'One of the most self-betraying things you can say to yourself is, "I really love doing that, but I can never make a living doing it so I am not going to do it."'

Marianne Williamson
Spiritual author and speaker

Most of us have been brought up to believe that we can either work for money and not enjoy it too much, or do something we love and pay for it by not earning much money. Can you relate to that? We often have deeply ingrained beliefs in the need for sacrifice: we have to sacrifice love for money, or money for love. We believe that the fulfilment of our responsibilities is not going to involve love and joy. But we can have both – love and money.

In June 2009, I found myself listening to Paul Potts, winner of the 2007 *Britain's Got Talent* TV show, when he was being interviewed by Steve Wright on BBC Radio 2. At the time Paul appeared on *Britain's Got Talent* he was making a living by selling mobile phones, but he astonished the show's judges and the audience with his incredible singing voice. Steve Wright asked Paul whether he had loved singing as a child, or whether he came to singing in later life. Paul responded, 'Yes, I'd always loved singing when I was young.' Steve asked him why, then, he had ended up selling mobile phones rather than singing professionally. Paul answered, 'No

one ever told me when I was growing up that something
I loved could be a career.'

Most of us can relate to that: getting paid for doing
something we loved simply wasn't a career option
that we were aware of, nor that we were encouraged
to follow when we were young. The thought simply
wasn't within the realms of our consciousness; we didn't
know it was possible. And, as it was not really present
in our minds, we never pursued it. But it has always
been possible for us and never more so than today. The
opportunities for making a living doing something we
love have never been more abundant than they are now.

The greatest scarcity lies in our thinking rather than in
the outside world. You may well have grown up with
some very limited ideas about the ways in which it is
possible to earn money. I therefore suggest that you
actively open your mind to the amazing variety of ways
in which you can earn money today and that you keep
your antennae alert to interesting people who positively
challenge your old beliefs.

A few years ago I was at a party where I got chatting
to a woman. I asked her what she did for her living, as
I often do. She responded by saying, 'I get paid to be
massaged.' I said, 'I'm sorry, I must have misheard you –
I thought you said you get paid to be massaged,' and she
replied, 'No, you didn't mishear me, I *do* get paid to be
massaged!'

I asked her how that worked and she explained that she
worked in a massage school, where part of the training
for the students involved her being massaged by them to
assess their competency. Now that blew my mind and
made me realise how much I limit myself through my
own beliefs about what I could be paid for!

Today, people are increasingly outsourcing their lives: because they don't have the skills or time that others have, they will bring those people in to help meet their own needs. We can be hired to do what they can't do or don't want to do. Some people are paid to sit in other people's homes, watch their TVs and eat their food – it's called house sitting. Others are paid to test duvets, chocolate, champagne and condoms. There is no area of human endeavour that people are not being paid for. It is possible to be paid for pretty much every area of human activity today. So before you dismiss any of your brilliant ideas by saying to yourself, 'But I could never get paid for *that*,' take a pause and do some research – and I am sure you will find that there are already lots of other people who are being paid to do precisely the thing you have thought of.

So ask yourself what, in your wildest dreams, you would love to be paid for doing or being. Because whatever activities you'd love to be paid for, there is a very good chance that there are people out there who would happily pay you to do it for them today.

Asking for and receiving money for doing work that is your art

'Your income is directly related to your philosophy, not to the economy.'

Jim Rohn
Motivational speaker and author

As we have already seen, since work is generally regarded as being something we'd rather not do, it feels natural to get money in return for our doing it. The money acts as a kind of compensation, a reward for spending our time, talent and energy in ways that we might not do otherwise. The money compensates us for the sense of sacrifice or pain that such work inevitably entails.

I often hear people say: 'Yes, I have found my calling now, but I am not going to pursue it until it's guaranteed to earn me the money I need.' But we can't demand that our calling pays. In some respects, our calling is not about money; it's a matter of our deeper soul, spirit and heart. We can nevertheless use cleverness, intelligence and talent to create income around it.

When we are doing what comes naturally to us – what we love and what intrinsically motivates us – our work will flow from us. However, we may initially be reluctant to regard this as an income source, or to ask for significant money in return for it, because it all feels too easy – almost like cheating. We may also think that money is somehow 'bad' and might taint the work we love. But it is possible for our work to be something very precious – and for it to remain precious even when we get paid for it and it becomes our business.

The motivation for the business you were born to create is likely to involve more of fulfilling a sense of purpose than simply a desire to make money. As an Inspired Entrepreneur, you will want to support yourself materially, but in a meaningful way. In some ways, the whole concept sits at 180 degrees to the traditional definition of business. By law, traditional businesses have to profit maximise for their shareholders. While Inspired Entrepreneurs are open to making big profits, they know this happens as a by-product of living their purpose, rather than because they set out to make money. They are so focused on helping and serving people, the money simply follows when they combine their intention with their skills.

The work you love isn't work in the conventionally accepted definition – i.e. something you'd rather not be doing. It's possible that you may actually feel guilty about asking for money for doing what comes naturally to you. But there is no reason for you to feel guilty. There is no divine law that says we can only receive money in return for experiencing pain. Nevertheless, as we have seen, the idea of receiving money in return for been happy, fulfilled, creative and joyful is not a familiar concept for everyone.

So check out your own attitude to see if there are any areas where you may be feeling guilty about your life being too good. Being happy and loving what you do is likely to lead to your success because it makes you attractive and draws people to you. Being happy is actually a signal that you are on track, and it will also draw the right people, situations, opportunities and resources to you.

Being entrepreneurial around what you love

'The money I have is in direct proportion to the value I've given to others. The more I give of myself, incredibly, the more economic power comes my way.'

Tod Barnhart
Author of The Five Rituals of Wealth

It is one thing to be good at what you do; it is another skill to create opportunities which will allow you to do what you love. So while one aspect of being an Inspired Entrepreneur involves the best possible delivery of what you do, another is being able to market yourself in order to find people to deliver your brilliance to. You need to become great at creating the opportunities to do what you love doing. You can do this by being passionate about serving people and making a difference. So make serving others your greatest joy and purpose.

I have come across too many people who, while they are willing to invest in their competence to deliver what they do, invest too little by comparison in learning how to find and attract clients for their work. They see this as 'selling themselves' and find it distasteful, rather than viewing it as a necessary means to find people who'd really love what they do and then to serve those people.

A great fear for many of us is that, once we take what we love and start turning it into a business, we'll need to become competitive, greedy, pushy and very money-driven. In fact, it is essential that we don't! It is possible to do what we love without becoming red in tooth and claw. The world doesn't need yet another impoverished person, so we need to earn an income doing what we love. This being the case, how do we attract clients, sell our products and services, and reach out to those who will benefit from our work?

Whilst passion and purpose are the crucial fuels behind doing what we love, two other factors are needed to create success:

- To be seen, known and trusted for doing what we love.
- To package what we love doing in a way that other people will want and need it.

As well as to love doing what we do, we need to be willing to keep getting better at doing it, and to be seen and to become known for doing it. In this way, people will find out about us, like our enthusiasm and hire us.

When you have a creative spirit, you also have an entrepreneurial spirit, although you may not realise it. Artists are by nature entrepreneurial – they're just not usually called this, and some of them may even resist the label because of our conventional ideas about what it means to be entrepreneurial. When looking at a canvas and imagining a painting, artists visualise something that doesn't yet exist. Inspired Entrepreneurs do something similar: they see the potential of an idea and how it could become a business. That's what makes them different from conventional businesspeople. Many businesspeople are essentially managers and administrators of what already *is* rather than creators of what *could be*. Inspired Entrepreneurs are by definition visionaries. The talents of Inspired Entrepreneurs and artists are interchangeable in many ways. However, many artistic people resist being business-like and dislike asking for money for their work – something which is not true of Inspired Entrepreneurs. To be successful doing what you love, you will need to become entrepreneurial, which in essence means looking for opportunities, creating opportunities and being enterprising.

There are some people who have been employed for much of their lives who find this transition particularly hard to make. In employed environments, the emphasis is often on just doing a job rather than on being actively enterprising. There is often a feeling of entitlement: we feel entitled to our salary for doing our job. However, artists and Inspired Entrepreneurs know they are not really entitled to anything.

I had a friend who left an academic environment to pursue his dream of teaching independently. He was absolutely brilliant at teaching, but I don't think he ever got used to the fact that he needed to create an audience for what he loved doing – he was so used to having people automatically turn up to his lectures and seminars in the university where he'd worked before. And, sadly, when he left he never created enough of an audience to generate the income he needed. He wasn't particularly entrepreneurial. He found it hard to show up – to bring his full commitment and presence to his work – to create the opportunities he needed to succeed.

My partner, Helen, loves designing and making jewellery from semi-precious stones and crystals. The time came when she had created quite a collection of pieces but she still hadn't shown them to anyone; it felt too risky for her to do in case her work wasn't given a warm reception. Then Helen asked if she could come along to one of my seminars and put her jewellery on display to get some feedback from the attendees. She was nervous but got some great comments, which helped her learn more about what women liked about her work, and she sold twelve bracelets. She was enterprising and showed up. Since that time in 2007, she has become even more enterprising and sold hundreds of bracelets and necklaces.

Being entrepreneurial means being active and consciously involved in becoming seen and known, as well as finding and creating opportunities for your work.

Doing what you love for free as a great strategy for getting paid

'A super, secret money insight, from your magician friend, The Universe... While great joy inevitably yields great abundance, rarely does this relationship work in reverse. But hey, at least you'll be rich. Dream of "the life", not the money. Because always, it's "the life" that draws the money, and not the other way around.'

Mike Dooley
Creator of Notes from The Universe

I am a massive advocate of showing up and doing what you love for free at first. The key is the 'showing up' part – because the money can't usually follow until you've shown up. You can't get paid *in theory* for something you haven't done *in practice*. I know I would not be where I am today, had I not been willing to show up for free at the beginning of my career and at various points since.

Here are nine reasons why I think you simply need to show up first in your work so that you can be paid for it in due course:

1. *You will enjoy yourself and step into your flow*. When you do what you truly love, you are in your flow; you are happier. When you love something, you simply

can't not do it. You and everyone else are blessed by that fact. Why would you rob yourself of this joy and pleasure? I would even go so far as to say that, if you are not doing what you love and thereby fulfilling your true purpose in life, you are likely to be drawn down into depression. The work you love is nourishing: you are brought to life by it and feel better for it. It can literally uplift and heal you.

2. *You will lower the initial emotional risk when you are willing to work for free to begin with.* When you do something new but there isn't any pressure on you to make it pay or deliver value for money, you are freed up to simply enjoy doing it and learn as you go. Doing something new while needing to earn your living from it at the same time can be a heavy weight to carry, and may involve trying to cross one too many thresholds at once.

3. *You will develop confidence.* Often you don't know how good you are at something until you actually do it. Don't wait to feel confident enough in order to get started, as confidence shows up when you actually get going. Once you begin something, you will receive positive feedback and appreciation; you will see yourself as others see you, rather than how you've judged yourself. You realise you are better than you told yourself you were, and you become more confident.

4. *You will build your skills.* You may have heard the expression 'every master was once a disaster', and it's true! Everybody who is great at what they do was once a beginner and not so good at it. So be prepared to take baby steps at first so that you can become good. Begin your apprenticeship and initiate the lifelong process of mastery.

5. *You will generate insights and ideas.* When you are actually in the flow, new insights and ideas will accrue, and you will evolve with your work. I am sure that one of the reasons my first book became a bestseller was because I gave talks on the subject, often for free, for seven years before I wrote a word of it. I had fielded hundreds of questions and refined my thinking accordingly before I began writing. And, as I gave talks, my inspiration generated new ideas that I could use in my book. At times, it may not always be clear at first how your passion could generate income, but if you increasingly do what you love anyway, you will receive suggestions and ideas on how to become paid to do it.

6. *You will create 'social proof', and establish credibility and opportunities.* When you do what you love, you will have impact and generate success stories and testimonials which demonstrate to others you are competent. Once you have demonstrated your competence, it won't matter that you weren't paid for your work at first – the reward at this stage lies in having shown you can produce results or solve problems.

7. *You will establish connections and build your audience.* When you show up, you create a certain resonance which means people will feel connected you – they will get to like, know and trust you. They can become a part of your tribe – your advocates – telling friends, family and colleagues about you. They will be interested in the other things you offer.

8. *You will send out a metaphysical message that you are truly committed.* Life responds to committed action rather than to planned commitment. Doing what you love brightens the world – it is an act of

service and an act of love, and because love is the fabric of life, I believe that life will move to support you and smooth your way. Your commitment initiates forces in unseen worlds.

9. *You will create opportunities when you show up.* When people witness you in your brilliance, your competence and your energy, they may well hire you – but they'll only hire you because you showed up. Around half the time I show up to do one thing, a door opens and I create an opportunity to do something else. By doing what you love consistently, you are likely to experience predictable miracles.

I am also an advocate of creating a clear boundary around how much you will do for free before you cross a threshold and start charging for your work. You need to value yourself and earn income so that what you do is a sustainable business. So don't work for pay at first, but be willing to do what you love for free, and then be willing to become well paid for your work.

Collaboration not competition

'I enjoy being given a certain amount of freedom in order to interpret or to come up with stuff, but I do enjoy collaboration. I seek and thrive on projects where I am going to learn from the people I'm working with.'

William Kempe
Actor

Many people who do what they love for a living find the language of traditional entrepreneurs off-putting: phrases such as 'blowing the competition out of the water' don't sit well with them. Their natural inclination is to co-operate; however, they may still have the idea deeply ingrained in their psyche that in order to survive they need to compete. That said, I believe we are entering a new age in business and that Inspired Entrepreneurs are at the cutting edge of this revolution. The key is this: the move away from a mindset of competition to a mindset of collaboration.

When we are inspired by a greater purpose, we'll find that many other people share that purpose with us. For example, say I want to live in a world where the majority of people do work they love, and are happier and more fulfilled in their work… to my mind, that's a lovely world to live in. And I know that thousands of other life coaches, writers, consultants and advisors share a similar purpose too. So, am I their competition? Or are they my competition?

From one perspective, yes they are. But I've thought about this carefully with my business partner, Niki, and we came to this conclusion: why not create a platform for sharing my ideas about work, business and Inspired Entrepreneurship, and then invite the best people out there, who are promoting similar ideas, to come and speak on our platform too? (See Section 5, 'Building your leadership platform', for more information on creating platforms.)

In doing this, inviting others to share our platform, we turned our potential competitors into collaborators. We now host a variety of speakers and authors who share their ideas and messages around our joint larger purpose – and it works brilliantly. Instead of competing we collaborate, and instead of fighting over slices of the cake, we bake a bigger cake so that there is more for everybody.

It does take a level of courage, self-belief and self-confidence to embrace the idea of a greater good, rather than just focusing on your own immediate good. But when you start moving from a win/lose mentality to a win/win mentality, the rewards can be enormous. Partnership and collaboration are the way forward – even collaboration with clients whom you might consider competition. Through collaboration we can create a bigger cake for everyone.

To plan or not to plan

'Pay less attention to resolutions and more attention to evolution.'

Alan Cohen
Author and spiritual teacher

Conventional business wisdom says that 'to fail to plan is to plan to fail'. Whilst there is some truth in that, I don't think it is the whole truth. I know many incredibly successful Inspired Entrepreneurs who have never made a business plan and who never intend to. They have dreams not plans. So if planning is not the whole picture, what else is involved in finding success? I believe the following things are important:

- An overriding sense of our purpose for being here, i.e. living our authentic calling.
- A vision and an idea of the right direction for our work and life.
- Consistent action and continuously taking steps, i.e. doing what lies before us today, tomorrow, next week...
- A willingness to show up every day with our gifts and talents, often in the face of fear and resistance.

In my experience, these things lead to personal evolution, and if you are a major part of your business, your own growth and evolution will be an integral ingredient of your success.

Here's what I believe after twenty years of running my own business and having helped hundreds of other

Inspired Entrepreneurs: there is a plan for you and for your business, but it is not written on shiny A4 paper in a lovely folder. It is more like a seed within your own heart and soul, waiting to come to fruition through you. Plan and commit to taking steps, take action and do what lies before you. This is a powerful use of your resources and your energy. But you don't need to know the whole plan from the outset; you just need to get into the momentum by taking the step ahead of you today in the confidence and knowledge that the plan will keep revealing itself to you as you keep on moving forward. You need faith and trust in life to keep moving forward in anticipation of results and successes.

Personally, I have a liking for projects. I tend to break down my evolution into a series of projects, such as writing a book, developing a new website, improving my understanding of social media or developing a new programme. For me, projects have boundaries, usually beginnings and endings, and often measurable and tangible results.

There is already an intelligence within you which is willing and able to guide you forward. You have an inner guidance system. Your business is a living entity and wants to work alongside you so that it can unfold. Your intuition and your inspiration will guide you forward – and a degree of planning can help this process along. Plans can reassure us when we lack confidence and help us to clarify our thinking, often stimulating good ideas. But a core belief that many of us have is that nothing will happen unless we plan meticulously for it to happen and then make it happen. This is based on the idea that we live in a mechanical universe which doesn't really care about us – and that just isn't true.

However, I do think that when we are setting out to create a business doing the work we love, we have to understand how much money we will need to bring in each month and what our costs are likely to be. We need to understand the practicalities, such as how email auto-responders work and ways to engage with social media to promote ourselves and our work. But, whatever the nature of our work, I think the key is this: *how* it is all going to happen will only become apparent as we create our own path.

We simply can't know all the details of the 'how' in advance. Creator of the daily 'Notes from the Universe' emails, Mike Dooley, calls this a case of the 'cursed hows'. He means that we often feed our resistance and don't take action because of our excessive need to know how things are going to turn out – *how* it will work. And understandably so. As we have seen, plans can help alleviate our fears. Sadly, though, I have met many people who have had fabulous plans, yet they have never taken any definite action to start their business and so have never even found their first client.

I don't think it is simply a case of planning or not planning – I think an Inspired Entrepreneur has a sense of both. An example of this is Jennifer Percival, who was a nurse in the NHS in the UK but who realised she wanted to create a bigger platform for herself. So she started by initiating her own projects and, ten years later, she now has her own fulltime business as an author and consultant, having become one of the world's expert nurses in smoking cessation. She told me, 'To this day, I don't have a formal business plan. I have continued to follow my heart and my inspiration. New and exciting opportunities open up each week. If I have an idea, I tell people about it. What I have noticed is that many of these shared "ideas" come back as offers of work. I have learnt to trust the process of creation and know that somehow it always works out just right.'

So you don't need to be a great planner to be a success. Jennifer is a highly grounded and practical woman. Like many Inspired Entrepreneurs, she has a great heart and is open to inspiration, guidance, and to moving forward in faith and trust. Inspired Entrepreneurs also have their feet firmly on the ground, and where necessary engage with spreadsheets and Internet strategies, cash flow and costings, but always from a place of authenticity. Success comes from a wonderful marriage of heart and head. They let their heart lead the way and figure out the 'how' as they go.

Another way to approach your own business development is to remain conscious of the fact that we live in an alive and interconnected Universe, which is inherently invested in supporting us as we grow into our full potential. That invisible but real forces are acting with you, within you and for you; that you are not alone, however much you may at times feel so. *A Course in Miracles* teaches us that: 'If you knew who walked beside you on your journey, fear would be impossible.'

Now I also think it is possible to be incredibly naïve and passive if we don't acknowledge the importance of our own role in creating the business we love and if we just sit back instead to let the Universe take care of the details. The obvious question is: 'How do I know when I am being naïve and stupid, or if I am moving forward in faith and trust?' If I am honest, there are times when I have prospered tremendously through my own faith and also other times when I have nearly gone bust through my own naivety. I think the best advice I can give you is to learn to trust yourself and develop confidence by increasingly trusting the intuitions of your own heart. There is an inner guidance system within you. Use it.

I do believe that there is an evolutionary impulse at work within the Universe, and within you. Might it not be possible that the Universe has a better plan for your happiness than you do? Things will eventually work out, but not always in the ways you plan them to. I think the Universe is less invested in giving you want you think you want, and more invested in teaching you that you are love, not fear. The more you remember that, the easier and more gracefully things will be for you.

Section 3:

Being an Artist and Creating Your Own Brand

The traditional model of work involves working for pay, in a job or career, and being largely motivated by rewards and punishments. But when we do what we love, we are intrinsically motivated – and this makes our work more like art than graft. Then we will want to do our best, and our art flows from us; it becomes the way in which we uniquely express ourselves and what we love doing. Love rather than money becomes our primary motivation for doing our work, although we are very willing to be paid – and even well paid – for doing it. When we really love what we do, it's possible to become our own uniquely brilliant brands and to be paid for our work.

Start thinking 'Brand You'

'A brand is a "trust mark". It's shorthand. It is a sorting device.'

Tom Peters
Author of The Brand You 50

It used to be that we chose a career, and then maybe changed career. And an employer would take care of us during that career. Today, it is much more important to take responsibility for your own work, career or business. Instead of focusing on what is going to make you employable or earn you lots of money, you may be asking yourself, 'What would I like to spend my days doing? And with whom? What sort of work makes me feel alive? And how can I get paid for doing it?' The shift is from survival-mode thinking to flourishing and knowing where your heart really lies – acknowledging what you are uniquely on this planet to do.

One of the best ways to approach this adventure is to start thinking of yourself as your own personal brand. By that, I don't mean becoming all veneer and no substance. True branding is about authenticity – it must convey the essence of who you are. By 'personal brand', I mean understanding yourself clearly and deeply, where your strengths lie, in what ways you can contribute most to the world; and then being able to communicate all of this clearly to others in order to persuade them to hire you or suggest that others hire you. Your followers and supporters are your gold – they should be precious to you and the heart of your business.

Start to think of yourself as 'You limited' (or 'You unlimited')! Begin to think of yourself as the *supplier* of your skills, experience, love, energy, insights, wisdom, talent, expertise and experience, rather than a potential employee who can offer these qualities. I think this is how the future of work will look: we will be the suppliers of our particular brand of brilliance for a number of clients who value and need what we are great at. For example, IBM recently announced that they are shedding around seventy per cent of their workforce in the next seven years, but will hire many of them back on a freelance basis as suppliers of their particular talents and expertise.

So start thinking of yourself in terms of your own personal brand, even if you've only ever been an employee until now. It becomes less of a question about you actually 'do' and more of a case of being able to tell authentic and interesting stories around what you have already done, and for whom – your signature projects, your 'wow!' projects in which you have shone and brought most value to clients and employers. You must package yourself – and include your personality in that package.

To create a powerful 'Brand You', it helps if you are noticeably good at doing what you love. Becoming a powerful and known personal brand means putting yourself out there, although initially it can feel really scary to be exposed in this way. So build up your profile from a place of purpose, with the clear intention of getting your message out there to be heard by as many people as possible; then shift your focus to those you can serve instead of yourself.

Today, it is more important than ever to be consistently hireable rather than to be merely employed or hired. This way of thinking will help you shift away from a mentality of dependency and the belief that you are reliant on others to create work opportunities for you. You will move into a place of greater interdependence, in which you realise that you are a supplier whose services can be hired by many others, either by employing you directly or by commissioning you through your own business. You will move into a place of greater equality and partnership.

To identify your own personal brand, answer the following questions:

- What do you stand for?
- What is your sense of purpose?
- What are your unique gifts and talents?
- What are your core values?
- What is your niche area of expertise?
- What are your 'wow!' projects?

Emotional connection is the heart and soul of 'Brand You'. As you become increasingly clear about this, you will build a reputation for successful projects; you will be employable and hireable, with an impressive track-record. You will accumulate a list of successfully completed 'wow!' projects on your CV, rather than of jobs or tasks.

Today it is projected that a significant number of us will change career many times during the course of our lifetimes – and that much of the work we will eventually do may not even exist yet in a form that we would currently recognise. Thinking of ourselves as brands will help us to keep on building on the shoulders of what we have already achieved and to carry on evolving as we face the future.

Your work as your art

'The true way to render ourselves happy is to love our work and find in it our pleasure.'

Françoise Bertaut de Motteville
French memoir writer

As we have seen, there is a subtle shift away from the idea of jobs and careers towards an appreciation of work as authentic creative expression. The concept of a 'job' emerged around the 1550s, when the word meant 'a piece of work' (in contrast to continuous labour); its origins were perhaps a variant of the word 'gobbe', meaning mass or lump. If a job was originally a lump, then no wonder that the very idea of one hasn't always seemed that appealing.

Similarly, we tend to have fairly narrow view of what 'art' means –writing, music, dance or painting may come to mind. But I believe that art is more about an attitude and a mindset rather than a means of expression, and think we could usefully broaden our concept of what art is.

Here are some of the differences between being a worker and approaching our work with artistry:

1. *Generally, people work for pay, but when we enjoy what we do and are intrinsically motivated, we work for something other than pay.* As artist Polly Morgan says, 'Even if people lost interest in my work and stopped buying it, I know I couldn't stop doing it. I have to do it to keep myself happy.'

2. *Work is often about routine whilst art is about evolution and progression.* Artists are always discovering new resources within themselves and expressing what they find.

3. *Workers tend to do work that is created by others, whilst artists create their own work.*

4. *Work is about doing the tasks that need to be done whilst artists want to be their best selves.* Doing their best work is therefore what is most important to them.

5. *Workers tend to value approval and conformity, whilst artists value brilliance and showing up in their work.*

6. *Artists create emotional capital through their work.* They create their following through goodwill, generosity and reputation.

7. *Work is often about following rules found in manuals and procedures, whereas artists follow their Muse.*

8. *Workers and artists have very different relationships to fear.* As workers, we might avoid fear, because it's just our job to carry out the tasks we do and we are not particularly invested in them emotionally. Artists, however, tend to be more invested emotionally in their work, and are constantly drawn in the direction of their fear so that they can grow and evolve.

9. *Artists love the process of becoming, whereas workers are often content to remain where they are.*

10. *Workers tend to do what they are paid to do, whilst artists enjoy sharing their gifts, regardless of money.* Artists love their engagement with people. The act of giving and sharing can be its own reward.

11. *Workers work for an employer; artists work for an ideal, a purpose, the greater good, as well as for themselves.*

12. *Workers tend to be motivated by external rewards like carrots and sticks, whilst artists are motivated intrinsically to do their work and are nourished by the very act of doing it.*

13. *Workers don't usually bring their genius to work, but artists are inspired by finding and expressing their genius.*

14. *Artists tend not to have precise job descriptions.*

15. *Workers are encouraged to fit in, whilst artists are comfortable standing out, being seen and becoming known for their work.*

16. *Workers often suppress and conceal their true nature to fit into their role, whereas artists love to explore and express their uniqueness.*

17. *Artists love evolving and improving on what they do.* Conventional work is often about doing the same stuff over and again.

18. *Art has the stamp of individual authenticity whilst work is usually a standardised commodity.*

19. *Workers need a map to follow, whereas artists are happier living without a map and discovering new territory as they go.*

20. Artists know that the way they approach their work can inspire people as much as their actual output.

Because artistry don't comply with manuals, rules or procedures, it isn't always easy for an artist to answer the questions, 'So how am I doing? How is my work?' There are fewer ways of measuring success as an artist than there are as a worker with quotas to fill. However, if your work is your art, there are two questions to ask yourself:

- How close to your own authenticity is your art?
- How close is your art to what you know you could express?

Authentic success cannot be measured just by satisfying the demands of our egos; it is also about fulfilling what our hearts and souls require of us. When we begin to think of ourselves as artists in our work, it is really important that we learn to listen more closely to our own sense of inner rightness and that we become better at self-validating our experiences, in addition to relying on the feedback of others.

People also want your energy

'When you work with love you draw others to you. Embrace this truth. The reason for this is that love is the highest vibration on earth. When you work with love people feel it, are helped by it and return to it. It's a positive vibration that draws people naturally into its sphere. Those who love what they do emote that love through their work, and are drawn towards their energy. That's why love is the best marketing tool around. Because it is so attractive, it pulls to you what you need.'

Sonia Choquette
Author of Your Heart's Desire

As well as our skills, expertise, insights and experience, people will be drawn to our unique energy. The more we inhabit ourselves and our individuality, the more we will develop presence and vitality. We embody this to the fullest when we are living our true calling, singing our souls' distinctive songs; when we are aligned with our inner selves, truly loving what we do and exuding love through all that we do. Your own brilliance is your competence illuminated by your inner light.

Our brilliance makes us attractive to people as it means that we've shown up authentically in our life and work.

People will want to be around that energy and bask in it. It enlivens and awakens something in them. And people will willingly pay for it. They will want your personality and your quirkiness as well as your skills; they will want something that comes from the heart and soul of you.

I love Bruce Springsteen and have been to his last two live concerts in London. But why am I willing to spend £100 on a ticket to hear his songs again, most of which I already know off by heart and can play any time I want to in the comfort of my own home? The reason is that being in the presence of such energy is an experience all of its own. To my mind, singing along with 30,000 other people to 'Born to Run' is a transcendent – even spiritual – experience, one that I simply do not get when listening to Bruce on my iPod, even with my best ear-buds! Author and spiritual teacher Alan Cohen writes: 'People will pay well to bask in the energy of someone fully alive and authentic in what they are doing, and rightfully so. Because we are spiritual beings at our core, it is the spirit in which we live that fulfils or undermines us. When you deliver the riches of your soul to your clients, you will uplift them and you will be well rewarded for your investment. Then everyone wins.'

People will pay for our energy when they see and experience its value – and when we get out of our own way, show up with it and let them pay us for it. A friend of mine told me how a client of hers decided he wanted to pay her double her stated fee right from the off, simply because he really wanted to work with her but didn't think she was charging enough. We could all do with some clients like that!

When we are coming from a place of high energy in what we do, we are usually giving full out, holding nothing back. The other side of this is a willingness to leave our own doors wide open to appreciation, love, gratitude, and, of course, money. Become a gracious receiver of all good things. So much can be given to us when we leave our doors open to receive. To do so also means embracing our own worth, our own significance and the impact we have on others.

Becoming your own brand is about developing your mastery of something and committing your energy to that process. It is about giving the world a clear picture of who you are and what you are great at. You are in charge of your life and you can make a difference to your clients' lives. You serve clients – that's what you do – so let people see how uniquely you can do this.

As an artist and entrepreneur, you initiate

'Very often audacity, not talent, makes one person an artist rather than a shadow artist – hiding in the shadows, afraid to step out and expose the dream to the light, fearful that it will disintegrate to the touch.'

Julia Cameron
Author of The Artist's Way

When our work has artistry in it, there is a tendency for us to be self-starters and take the lead in what we do. We just go do things, we show up; we make things happen when others are hiding out from fear – we simply find it hard not to. We actively look for work that needs doing and for fresh opportunities, rather than sit around waiting for instructions or permission from someone else. We initiate, our ideas and art bubble up from within us and seek expression. But there are a number of ways to be and to act in the world:

1.   To be passive and not act at all.

2.   To wait for instructions to act.

3.   To react to circumstances.

4.   To respond to circumstances.

5.   To initiate and cause things to happen.

There is a subtle difference between reacting to and responding to circumstances. By 'reacting', I'm referring to what is usually an unconscious habitual way of behaving when something happens to us or around us; whereas responding to circumstances involves pausing and thinking about the options for action, and then choosing the optimal response. To initiate and cause things to happen usually involves taking action based upon an inner calling rather than external circumstances. It means choosing our own trajectory and taking responsibility.

In my experience, most people follow instructions, react and respond – whether it is to the economy, to colleagues, to their competitors, to the recession, to shareholders, to legislation. Fewer people initiate through their deeper sense of calling. It takes courage to initiate. No one is necessarily making us do anything, but something inside ourselves calls us to. I think that many people have trouble taking responsibility. It is often easier to say 'they made me', or 'I had to', or 'I had no choice'. It takes guts to say, 'I choose to' and then not to feel you have to justify yourself.

I am a great admirer of people who make self-initiated changes and I'm very glad that I've done this myself in the past. When I changed from my corporate career to running my own business, there were no external forces making me take that step, which made me think I must be a little mad. The only forces calling me to initiate change came from deep inside me. Often we wait until we are ill, in great pain, or things fall apart, to make changes so that we can then justify our need to change.

Either inspiration or desperation is usually the motivating factor in creating change, so make a conscious decision to be willing to change in your work and business because you are inspired rather than despairing. 'The smart horse gallops at the shadow of the whip' says the line from the poem; become more awake and aware, and give yourself permission to initiate change. Don't wait until things get really bad.

Initiating change puts you in charge of yourself and your environment. It means that you have sovereignty over your own decisions – and that is a powerful place in which to be.

I think 'entrepreneurs in training' – people who work in organisations but actually have a strong entrepreneurial spirit within them – often have a hard time. They can see how things could be done better and more effectively in their employment, and they have no trouble initiating change. But the fact that they keep suggesting changes, and thereby inadvertently questioning the status quo, often gets them branded as trouble-makers. When their great gift – initiating positive change – is seen as a weakness and a flaw by their employer, they may end up believing there is indeed something wrong with them personally.

Most of the Inspired Entrepreneurs whom I know and with whom I have worked are initiators. They are positive-change agents, dreamers and doers, philosophers and men and women of action, who live their spirituality in what they do and how they live. They don't need to be given permission to act; they have a fire of inspiration alight within them and they keep stoking that fire. They are self-starters and don't need an external boss to get them motivated.

You have access to genius and brilliance

'In the middle ages the belief changed from having a genius to being a genius – that was huge error. The pressure of that has been killing artists for the last 500 years. Can we return to some different relationship between humans and the creative mystery? How can we relate to it without losing our minds?'

Elizabeth Gilbert
Author of Eat, Pray, Love

Genius is an overused word, and yet I still believe that there is genius within you. Actually, more precisely I think you have *access* to genius. It is not necessarily resident within you, but you are able to approach it. When you are divinely inspired – via your Muse, your guardian angel, God or whatever power you believe in – your genius will lie at the heart of your artistry and your personal brand. One of the strongest characteristics of genius is the power of lighting its own fire and of self-initiation, and the core of genius is authenticity. Interestingly, the words 'genius' and 'genuine' ultimately derive from the same Latin root word, 'gen', relating to people or a group.

Throughout history, people have understood that there are external forces of inspiration. The Greeks believed that each person had their own *daimon* – a spirit or divine power; the Romans believed in the Muses, forces greater than the individual psyche. According to the Ancients, these were the true sources of genius. Today, when we show up creatively we may feel ourselves inspired by greater forces too. We may feel that we are not necessarily the source of our own genius, but act as willing partners to it. We access genius when we are true to our inner spirit, our own particular calling and vocation.

A more precise derivation of the word 'genius' than its root word 'gen' is actually the Latin term *genius*, which can refer to the guardian spirit of a person or a household, to somebody's spirit, inclination, wit or inborn nature. If we think of genius as being like a household guardian spirit, we might liken it to a being such as Dobby the house elf in *Harry Potter and the Chamber of Secrets*. The job of our genius is to sprinkle ideas and magic on us and our projects. Strange and unscientific as that sounds, this fits the model of creativity that most artists and Inspired Entrepreneurs describe. Artists and Inspired Entrepreneurs show up, they are inspired, they experience resistance, they keep going and then they give birth to some form of creative gift or project.

A few hundred years ago, we largely did away with our belief in forces such as the Muses and *daimons*, and focused on human beings instead as the source and centre of the universe. But it can be a heavy burden to believe that you are the source of your own genius – to be labelled as one and then required to deliver on that expectation. I don't think it is too much of a stretch to attribute much of the self-destruction of many creative people over the last two hundred years to their inability to deal with that heavy burden.

We tend to think of artists as emotionally unstable. However, we all have demons, baggage and anxieties, but the trick is in controlling them. Similarly, we all possess optimism, gifts and spirit, and the trick is in tapping into them. By taking one step back and allowing yourself to access genius, it will come to you more easily. Although genius won't immunise you from hard work, there will be a different quality to the effort involved. It will no longer be such a struggle; instead, you will increasingly find yourself in a state of flow in your work as you begin to immerse yourself in your natural element.

Recognise your inner resistance to your work as art

'Rule of thumb: the more important a call or action is to our soul's evolution, the more resistance we will feel toward pursuing it.'

Steven Pressfield
Author of The War of Art

Another of the great dynamics that will determine your success in starting your own business is not your talent, the quality of advice you receive, your business plan or your credentials: your success will also be determined by your capacity to recognise, understand and overcome your inner resistance to giving birth to your entrepreneurial dreams.

In my experience, the things we most want to do deep in our hearts are often the very things that we feel most scared and conflicted about when it comes to taking action. As our potential for authenticity and fulfilment in our work increases, so the emotional stakes rise, often causing us either to shift sideways into something less authentic and safer, or to stop ourselves completely.

As you choose to move closer to living a more inspired and heartfelt life as an Inspired Entrepreneur, it is possible that you will begin to experience forces within yourself that try to hold you back. However powerful your soul's call to your self-realisation is, there will be potent forces of resistance arrayed against your deeper self. Resistance is about how you conspire against yourself and your potential, and how you undermine your own efforts to create a more exciting and authentic life. Your resistance may have been within you for a long time, although it may only surface now as you start to move towards realising your true potential, because most resistance operates out of our awareness.

Resistance is what stands between the life you are living now and your unlived life – your life as it could be. It is essential to understand the nature of resistance. What may at first seem strange is that the more important a call, project or action is to you and your personal evolution, the more resistance you are likely to feel towards pursuing it. Yes, it sounds crazy, but it is a dynamic that is most people I know and work with will encounter at some point in their lives. It is what I personally have experienced. All of us have these twin forces within us: inspiration and resistance. It can often feel like our power to resist is greater than our power to follow through on our inspiration. However, we can all learn to overcome and beat our resistance.

You should understand there is unlikely ever to be a day when you can make a start on fulfilling your dreams just because you no longer feel any resistance. If you are waiting for that day, you could have a long wait! A large part of your success will follow from your willingness to act in the face of your resistance, and not by meekly waiting for your resistance to subside. You cannot overcome resistance theoretically, but only by actually doing what you are afraid of. As Eleanor Roosevelt famously said, 'You gain strength, courage, and confidence by every experience in which you really stop to look fear in the face. You must do the thing which you think you cannot do.'

Understand your resistance

'The difference between successful people and those less successful, is that successful people keep moving ahead even when voice of self-doubt chides them to stop or go back.'

Alan Cohen
Author and spiritual teacher

Each of your pioneering efforts is likely to be met with resistance, so to become a successful Inspired Entrepreneur, it is important that you understand these three things:

1. The fact that resistance exists and the ways in which it operates.

2. How resistance is likely to operate in your life and what purpose it seeks to serve.

3. How to beat your resistance by 'turning pro'.

You are probably no stranger to resistance. If you have ever bought an exercise bike and then hardly used it, had an idea for a book but never written it, or have wanted to start your entrepreneurial venture for years but not yet done so, then you're already familiar with resistance. It is that inner inertia – those feelings of fear, doubt, anxiety or unworthiness which arise when you want to move forward towards what you truly wish to do. Those feelings are normal, so don't worry: there is absolutely nothing wrong with you if you experience them!

As with most changes in life, the first stage is simply to become aware of your resistance to change. You need to be aware of how resistance operates so that you can see how it operates in your own life. Resistance is likely to be there already, although you may not become fully aware of it until you decide to take steps to live a more authentic life. Resistance usually shows up most forcefully when we move towards something that is personally meaningful to us, like starting our dream business.

Even as you read this, you may well be having some insights into your behaviour and perhaps even cringing a little as you see your own inner workings being laid out. It is important that you don't use your new insights about your resistance as a reason to be harsh with yourself – that would just feed your resistance further. Accept that resistance is part of the territory of being human, and that we're all subject to it. Now, you are actively becoming more aware of it and are choosing to make something else – your entrepreneurial dreams – more important than your resistance.

Understand how your resistance shows up

'Show me someone who has done something significant and worthwhile, and I'll show you someone who has most likely overcome resistance.'

Lou Holtz

Football coach, sportscaster, author, and motivational speaker

Perhaps it might help you understand what I mean by resistance if I explain that every book I have written (including this one), every seminar I have created, every broadcast I have made, has required me to face, engage with and overcome a degree of resistance. I know many people subscribe to a myth that goes like this: successful people obviously don't experience resistance, because otherwise they wouldn't be successful. I think the truth is more likely that many people succeed because they learn to recognise their resistance and then they learn how to overcome it. They feel doubts and insecurities, but show up anyway.

So what does resistance look like and how does it manifest itself in your own life? Some of the most obvious ways in which resistance to starting a dream business can show up are:

- By saying to yourself, 'I can't be bothered' or 'what's the point?' You are reluctant to invest energy in moving things forward.

- Procrastination: you are going to do it one day, but now's never quite the right time. There's always a reason not to proceed.
- Self-sabotage: you don't follow through on the opportunities that come your way.
- Living a 'shadow life': you keep aspects of your own creativity and talent on the sidelines of your life, and support other people's success and talent instead.
- Rationalisation and excuses: you are always sure why something won't work out or why you couldn't do it. You become an expert on pitfalls and know what all the potential problems might be, so decide it's safest not to go ahead with your plans after all.
- Talking yourself out of it: you consistently talk yourself out of the very thing you are drawn to.
- Excessive busyness: you don't make the time or conserve the energy you need to pursue what you'd love to do.
- Fear of judgement and excessive need for approval: the fear of doing anything that might jeopardise the love and approval you receive from others.
- Too much emotional drama: you always find yourself embroiled in fights, power struggles or arguments that drain your energy, or you are constantly outraged at others' behaviour.
- Waiting to feel 'good enough'.
- Addictions: any addictive behaviour that regularly stops you doing what you love.
- Being a perpetual student: studying what you love but never becoming a practitioner of what you have learned.
- Being a perpetual researcher: you acquire ideas and information but you never take the decision to act on them.
- Isolation: you don't acquire the support, encouragement and help you need.

- Focusing on past mistakes or failures, and fearing their repetition.
- Being excessively harsh and punitive towards yourself: you beat yourself up for your past mistakes or failures.
- Excessive dreaming and fantasising: you spend a lot of time thinking but never actually acting.
- Telling yourself 'littleness' stories, e.g.: 'who am I to do something like that?' and then putting yourself down.
- The anticipation of shame for thinking you could achieve anything significant.
- Building castles in the air: you make wonderfully exciting plans for your hugely successful businesses, but you never actually doing anything with them or find your first client.
- Discouragement: you allow yourself to be deterred by the advice or opinions of others.
- Being unrealistic: you are initially over-enthusiastic but are impractical about the timescales and the commitment required, then crash and burn out quite quickly.
- Lack of commitment: you start projects but then move on to new ones before finishing those you have already started.

I am sure you can recognise a number of the activities listed above as ways in which you too resist pursuing your dreams. Be aware that resistance can also hijack everyday activities and turn them into distractions and avoidances. For example, if every time you get ready to start writing your book, you find that you begin cleaning the house, surfing the Internet, decorating or re-arranging your wardrobe, then you can be sure that your inner resistance is at work.

Section 4:

Being a Pro in your Work and Business

As we saw in Section 3, most people who do the work they love will experience some resistance around it, because the emotional stakes are so high. To do the work we love, we have to put ourselves out there, truly and authentically, and risk success and failure, appreciation and criticism. The door to success can be opened by turning professional, which means deciding to commit to doing what we love in the face of our fear and resistance. We choose to make something greater and more important than our fear and resistance; we invest less energy in excuses and delays, and more in actually doing our work and creating the life and business we want.

Turning pro is your choice to cross a threshold

'Being a professional is doing the things you love to do, on the days you don't feel like doing them.'

Julius Erving (aka Dr J)
Retired American basketball pro

I would like to acknowledge Steven Pressfield for inspiring my thinking in this section of the book. In *The War of Art*, Steven suggests that there is a way of beating resistance which he calls 'turning pro'. When we think of 'being a pro', we tend to think of someone with formal qualifications in a paid occupation, such as a dentist, doctor, banker or lawyer. An amateur, on the other hand, is someone who works for the love of what they do, but who is not necessarily sullied by money. However, being a true pro has nothing to do with whether or not we earn money. Instead, it is an attitude towards our calling, our work and towards making good on our souls' promise. When you love your work so much that you want to place it at the centre of your life – rather than approach it like an amateur, who keeps it at the periphery of his or her life, only doing it 'for fun' at evenings and weekends – then you know you are a pro or that you are ready to turn pro. By making your work your vocation rather than an avocation, you make a commitment to it that the amateur fears making. As a pro, you work for love, but are willing to be paid for your work so that you can keep devoting yourself to it and sharing your gifts.

At the heart of turning pro lies something simple but immensely powerful. The pro says: 'I love my work, and I want to be able to do it full time. So I commit to my work and I commit to recognising my resistance around it; and I will act in the face of my resistance every day so that I can do my work every day.' The pro is fully aware that there are no certainties about how everything is going to turn out. But making the commitment to work, and to mastering it, means that the pro *will learn* how to make it succeed. As a pro, you commit to doing your work and to being entrepreneurial around it, thereby serving your god or gods – or your genius if you like. In essence, you deliver your work in progress; you complete and ship your projects as an ongoing process, rather than wait for everything to be perfect before dispatch.

There is no magic to turning pro. It is simply a choice we can make as an act of will. It is often a choice that is made most powerfully when we have had a taste of something that resonates with our soul. Then we may feel a new future beckoning us, a world in embryo within us that wants to be made manifest through us.

In 1985, when I worked selling expensive computers to Japanese banks, I began to hear my calling clearly. An interest in personal and spiritual growth was awakened in me as I read certain books, attended various workshops and went into therapy for my own benefit. By 1986, I felt I had come home to myself and found my vocation.

I gave my first talks and began to immerse myself in my new work during my spare time. But it took me another four years before I made the decision to turn pro and commit myself to leaving my corporate job and starting my own business. My resistance was huge. My initial attitude was one of five per cent inspiration, five per cent self-belief and five per cent self-confidence, compared to eight-five per cent doubt, anxiety, self-questioning and at some points downright terror. But nevertheless I took the decision to go for it, to turn pro, and I quit my secure corporate job.

Boy, there have been some ups and downs along the way! Times when I've felt my heart would burst with joy for the fun I'm having; when it all feels so meaningful and I'm completely happy. Times when my own resistance has felt so immense I've believed it might overwhelm me. But that spark of the pro in me has kept me moving forward. Before long, I knew that I couldn't go back; that to do so it would kill my soul. I knew I could only move forward, becoming more intelligent, wiser and smarter about the work I love to do, and more committed to following my Muse rather than allowing myself to be held back by my fears.

Today, in 2010, I am doing better than ever. There are still some ups and downs, but I wouldn't swap the adventure of it for anything. My work has brought me to the place where I dreamed to be, and I have always known I've been living my own authentic life along the way – and that to me is the greatest success of all. I have a much happier relationship with myself.

Ultimately it is your relationship with yourself which will determine everything – how much success, love, money, gratitude and appreciation you'll allow into your life. Stop for a moment and think about what you enjoy doing. In what areas of your work and life are you being called to turn pro?

As a pro, you make clear choices

'The thing that cowardice most fears is a decision.'

Søren Kierkegaard
Danish philosopher and religious writer (1813–55)

Most Inspired Entrepreneurs are at heart artists. They know they have work – or works – to do: an Inspired Entrepreneur has gifts to share, a person to become and a destiny to fulfil. We often experience a deep nagging feeling when we know we have gifts that we are not sharing; and, interestingly, most artists understand that they will not feel complete until they are giving their talents. Their mode of operation is opposite to that of received wisdom. Artists know they have something to do and that they've just got to do it, even if no one is watching them or paying them to do it. But then hopefully they will figure out how they can get paid for it. As Maya Angelou said so eloquently, 'Don't make money your goal. Instead, pursue the things you love doing, and then do them so well that people can't take their eyes off you.'

In Section 3, we saw how we can take the decision as an artist or an Inspired Entrepreneur that we are going to pursue our calling rather than just sell our time in exchange for money. Most professional artists will tell you that they've been through tough times when their art didn't bring in much of a financial reward. In pursuing the work we love, we may have to give up some things for a while to help tide ourselves over, but ultimately it will be worth it. There are greater rewards to be gleaned.

Perhaps one of the toughest and most empowering choices you can make as a pro is to start reassessing the value you once placed in the stories and excuses you've told yourself and the world about why you couldn't do the work you love. There will always be a stack of socially acceptable reasons as to why you can't pursue your dream right now: the recession, too little time, not enough qualifications, too many pressures and responsibilities, not enough money or support, lack of preparation, not feeling confident enough or adequate enough. And all of these considerations will have some truth to them.

However, your work will persist in calling to you. As you continue to listen closely to its call, you may find yourself gradually investing more in your work than in your stories and excuses. You will cross a threshold and – once you experience the joys and fulfilment of being a functional artist and Inspired Entrepreneur – you will be willing to abandon the seeming safety of your stories and excuses, and there will be no turning back for you. At this stage, you've made something else greater and more important than your fear.

As a pro, you act in anticipation of inspiration

'Inspiration does exist, but it has to find you working.'

Pablo Picasso
Artist (1881–1973)

I think one of the most important distinctions that an Inspired Entrepreneur pro understands, that other people don't, is this: often we may not feel inspired to do our work, but by doing it we become inspired. We often have to cross a threshold to find inspiration and enter the flow of our work – but that is exactly what our resistance doesn't want us to do. We can initiate inspiration by confronting our fears and simply getting on with our work.

The writer William Somerset Maugham was once asked whether he wrote when inspiration struck him or at any particular times. He answer was simple and profound: 'I sit down to write at nine o'clock each day and I find that inspiration strikes me about five past nine every day.' I believe he meant that every day he knew he would come up against resistance, such as reasons why he shouldn't write or not feel like writing. But he was a pro and defied his resistance by sitting down to write anyway. In that process of crossing his threshold, he opened the door to his Muse and ideas started to flow for him.

There will be days when we don't feel like working, but the more pro we become, the more we will do our work anyway and get into our flow. There is a part of us all that is both aware of resistance and determined not to succumb to it. Part of us will remain wise enough to keep an eye on the rewards that lie just on the other side of our resistance.

Sometimes our actual work isn't that difficult – in fact, it may even be easy – but our resistance to doing it can nevertheless be massive. Sometimes I still feel terrified when I stand up to give a talk but within minutes I am in my flow and loving it. Likewise, I can avoid writing for days, but when I do sit down it often just pours through. Apparently, even in his seventies the actor Henry Fonda could still sometimes be sick with fear before he went on stage, but he would go on stage anyway and give great performance.

Remember, the goal of resistance is to stop you from doing your work, to stop you from ever getting into your flow, because it knows that when you get in the flow of the work you love, it will have lost its power over you. Resistance hates it when we turn pro and commit to showing up in our work, because this means that it has lost its control over us.

As a pro you work for love, but are paid for your work

'We are all born carrying a promise – a promise to make the world better – and there's a yearning to make good on that promise that none of us can suppress forever.'

Marianne Williamson
Author of The Age of Miracles

The traditional view is that we work for pay. I guess that the majority of people might not do the work they do if it weren't for their need of money. But Inspired Entrepreneurs have different motivations.

When you are an artist at heart and run your own business doing what you love, your work will be intrinsically fulfilling and nourishing. It's ingrained in your heart and soul to do it; it's literally what you are here for. You enjoy doing it and you may even harbour a sneaky suspicion that at times you would even be willing to pay to do it, because you feel so blessed in connection with it. But in my experience this sensation can create its own problems for some of us. Because you happily and readily do your work, and might even be willing to pay for the opportunity that allows you to do it, you might then find it hard to ask consistently for money in return for doing it. Obviously, if you find it easier to give away what you do than to charge for it, this could make it tricky for you to run a sustainable business!

As we discussed in Section 2, the key is this: don't work for pay, but be willing to be paid for your work. This is a subtle but powerful distinction. It returns you to the heart of your work, to what you love doing and to an attitude of service. You are doing your work for great reasons. And so that you are able to sustain your work, you are willing to ask for and receive money in return for it.

As we have already seen, one big obstacle you may need to overcome will be guilt. In twenty years of consulting in this area, I have observed that feeling guilty about asking to be paid for work that we love and enjoy can be a real obstacle when it comes to running a successful and prosperous business. In contrast, when we have made sacrifices and suffered by doing work we don't particularly enjoy, we don't feel so guilty about receiving money in return for it. But money doesn't need to be a 'compensation' for the time we dedicate to our work; it is simply what we choose to receive in return for our goods and services.

The poet, singer and songwriter Leonard Cohen has been an artist for forty years; to my mind, he expressed it beautifully when he said, 'I always thought I was in my career as an artist for the long haul. I was able to satisfy the only dictum I set up for myself – I didn't want to work for pay, but I wanted to be paid for my work. I was able to achieve that, and that's an incredibly lucky turn of events.'

I love that idea: don't work for pay, but do be paid for your work. It is a perfectly possible goal to realise, and never more so than today. So make that your dream and your aim. Separate your work from the idea of money; do your work primarily because it's motivated by your heart and then use all your intelligence to figure out who'll pay you to do it for them.

As a pro, you have a different relationship with fear

'Pursue your dreams not because you're immune to heartbreak, but because your real life, your whole life, is worth getting your heart broken a few thousand times.'

Martha Beck
author, speaker and coach

I would love to be able to say to you that following your heart, doing what you love and creating a business around it, will be easy for you – that you'll get a free pass and never have to experience any difficulties, fear or obstacles. But I can't say that. In fact, at times it may be the opposite: you will have to encounter some of your greatest fears. That is the bad news, but there is also good news. Where you feel most discomfort and your limiting beliefs start to scream out loud in your head is also where you are most alive and where your greatest growth can occur. The precise areas that you fear the most can be the greatest birthing places of your potential.

It is helpful to remember three things:

1. *Fear and resistance is generally a pointer.*
    Remember, the more important a calling or project is to you, the more likely you are to experience fear. So in the course of doing the work you love, you

will be called to do some of the things that scare
you most; you will need to look fear in the face
and act anyway in pursuit of your highest self and
greatest good.

2. *There are resources within you and available to you
    which are greater than your fears.* You are greater
    than the sum of your fears. It may take you years
    to grow bigger than them and for them to have less
    hold over you. Yet what you face and overcome, you
    become inoculated against. Remember that on the
    other side of each of your fears lies another aspect
    of your own freedom.

3. *Although you may fear failure, looking stupid, falling
    on your face, no longer belonging or no longer
    being loved and approved of, your greatest fear
    relates to none of things.* Strange as it may sound,
    what probably scares you more than anything else
    is the prospect of becoming your greatest self and
    realising just how successful, talented and brilliant
    you could be. This is often a fear we hide even from
    ourselves. But just imagine for a moment going to
    your local bar, or a family gathering, and saying to
    all assembled: 'I'm really happy, truly fulfilled; I'm
    making sacks full of money, have people queuing
    up to work with me, am receiving tons of accolades
    and my family are all doing brilliantly too.' What
    kind of reception do you think you'd receive? It can
    take real courage to allow your life to be really good
    and blessed, and I believe it's an act of love and
    leadership when you do. But you'll always find that
    there are some people who are jealous of you, who
    begrudge you and who may even downright attack
    you for your achievements, perhaps even saying that
    your success shows you are immoral.

We all have places in which we feel confident and places that we fear. The journey of the Inspired Entrepreneur can be a great, practical and vibrant way to increase those areas where we feel confident by facing and relinquishing our fears. Fears come in many shapes and sizes, some logical and some illogical. All of them come from our neurosis and personalities, but the deepest part of us – the wholeness within us – doesn't know fear, and is immune from ever being able to feel fear. That core part of us is solid.

As you face your fears, you will gradually transform them into confidence. In every spiritual tradition there is a belief in an alchemical power or force that can do for us what we can't achieve for ourselves. This power can help us relinquish our fears when we can't do it on our own.

As a pro, you understand the incredible power of baby steps

'Opportunities come to those who dare. As we risk taking the next right step, the universe surprises us with its support.'

Julia Cameron
Author of The Artist's Way

The vast majority of people dream of their working lives being more exciting and inspiring, but they often don't move beyond the dreaming stage. The greatest power at our disposal is our ability to take action in the direction of our dreams – even in the form of tiny little baby steps which we may not initially see the point of taking. It is so easy to become caught up in an 'all-or-nothing' mentality, which is a form of resistance. Our dreams are only ever made manifest one little step at a time. Baby steps can break us out of a frustration loop when we feel exasperated that things aren't as we want them to be, yet we can't make major changes.

What you may not fully understand is the power behind your baby steps. Like a yacht that raises its sails to catch the wind, your baby steps can capture greater forces. My friend Mike Dooley, creator of the daily 'Notes from the Universe' email series, puts it this way: 'You don't take baby steps for the distance they cover, but to put yourself in the receivership of life's magic.' As you take baby steps, the Universe gets behind you.

I am not talking about turning yourself into a manic, mad person who never sits still; I am great fan of silence, stillness, prayer and mediation. Rather, it's about those moments when you may have a big idea and take a small step in pursuit of it, then another and another one step at a time: doors open, synchronicities occur, opportunities arise.

I could tell you hundreds of stories about baby steps working for me and for the people I know. One of my favourites happened in 2004, when I was invited to give a talk at a new organic food and health show, which was taking place that September in Alexandra Palace, near to where I lived in north London. Having accepted the invitation, I heard from colleagues that they thought the event wasn't going to be a great success. As the day arrived, it was raining and miserable, and I wondered to myself, 'Is it even worth going? I'm not being paid, my talk is only a couple of hours after the show opens and there will probably be hardly anyone there. Why am I bothering to do this?' My resistance kicked in, and I nearly talked myself into staying home, but I drove there nevertheless to give my talk.

And I was nearly right! As I stood up to give my talk at midday, there were about four people and a dog waiting to listen to me. It was noisy as there wasn't a dedicated area for talks, and people were constantly milling past. Again, I felt justified in abandoning it. But I persevered and gave the forty-five-minute talk anyway. By the end of it, the audience had swelled to twenty, and the dog had wandered off. I think I sold one book, but I noticed that once I'd got going I'd thoroughly enjoyed myself, and I was reminded of just how much resistance can prevent you from showing up to do your work.

Then a nice American lady came over to introduce herself to me. 'Hi, I'm Shari,' she said, 'and may I introduce you to Mr Kessler?' She gestured towards the distinguished-looking gentleman at her side. 'He founded and owns a vitamin and health food company based in New York. We enjoyed your talk, and we have our annual sales conference in California in January. We wondered if you might be interested in coming to give a similar talk for us at our conference?'

Fast forward four months, and I am arriving at Santa Barbara Municipal Airport, being picked up by limousine and taken to a stunning 2,000-acre ranch near Santa Ynez, close to where Michael Jackson used to live. There, I was looked after wonderfully, spent two nights on the luxury ranch, gave a two-hour talk, was appreciated and then paid handsomely, and then enjoyed a couple more days hanging out with friends who lived nearby.

This demonstrates the power of showing up to do and be what you are inspired by and passionate about!

Baby steps are so powerful because it takes the mystery out of success – we all have it in our power to take baby steps each and every day. And paradoxically, when we take baby steps, we initiate wonderful, magical and miraculous forces to speed our way, and we grow in confidence and competence.

To become a true pro, get a few failures under your belt

'I have always grown from my problems and challenges, from the things that don't work out, that's when I've really learned.'

Carol Burnett
Actress, comedienne, singer, dancer and writer

So many people treat failure like it's going to be their personal undertaker, marking the very end of them – involving an emotional death if not a literal one. But until we have experienced a significant failure or two, we are likely to live in the shadows of failure. Part of our mind will be forever worrying about the possibility of failing, and doing all we can to avoid this. We may even avoid being as authentic as we could be, for fear of being rejected or judged. We are all likely to censor ourselves in subtle and often unconscious ways in order to receive approval or create success. To avoid risking failure, we may hold back from doing something close to our heart, whereas committing ourselves wholeheartedly could create success.

I am not suggesting that you go out and act recklessly in order to experience failure! But I am suggesting that you have the courage to go beyond what is familiar to you, to listen to your inner voice, and to act and show up in ways that feel scary yet authentic for you. Sometimes this will be productive and create opportunities. At other times, it won't always work out. Then, you may well feel disappointed, even gutted, but you will get over it, lick your wounds and learn valuable lessons from the situation.

Very few people enjoy failure, but in all likelihood we will experience our greatest successes after a few setbacks, as long as we keep going. We will liberate ourselves in the long term by facing our fears and realising that, far from being the death of us, they can actually be doorways to greater freedom. When we are afraid of failure, then fail but survive, we become stronger, free and more confident. Freedom is about not being restricted by fear, and is often achieved by facing and moving through our fears.

If you explore the narratives of some of the people you most admire, you'll find that many of them will have had failures along the way. Often their greatest successes have come after various failures. Mariana Caplan expressed this beautifully in her book *The Way of Failure: Winning Through Losing*: 'We are not taught how to fail and how to lose with dignity and awareness. Our so-called and imagined failures become the doorway to profound success in our lives – success that is not measured by commonplace standards, but by the currency of depth of being, compassion and wisdom. The very experiences, events and emotions we fear most and attempt to avoid are frequently our greatest opportunities – openings we often pass up because our apprehension keeps us from learning to experience failure in such a way that it is transformed into invaluable gain.'

Pros self-validate and develop a professional core

*'The professional endures adversity. He
lets the birdshit splash down on his slicker,
remembering that it comes clean with a heavy
duty hosing. He himself, his creative centre,
cannot be buried, even beneath a mountain of
guano. His core is bullet proof. Nothing can
touch it unless he lets it.'*

Steven Pressfield
Author of The War of Art

As you move into the realm of work as art, you will find that there are fewer rules to follow, fewer ways of being externally validated. Your journey then is to become more and more self-validating. You will need to develop your inner validation system so that you know you are in harmony with your authentic self.

Let's compare the differences between being a hack and being an artist. A hack is someone whose major pre-occupation is: 'what's going to make me money and make me popular?' So a hack seeks validation from the market and only works on whatever they think the market will go for. However, an artist produces whatever she or he is inspired to do, and then brings that to market.

A hack uses the market and sales as forms of validation. Hacks want whatever the market appears to want. Their sense of self-worth is based to a large degree on a sense of their reception and achievements in the market place. Whereas an artist looks within and asks, 'Is this my best and most authentic work? Am I being true to myself?' And only the artist can answer that question.

Artists gradually learn to self-validate – to create work that has authenticity in their own eyes and which expresses who they really are. They then bring that work to market. They don't continually seek the opinion of others. Picasso didn't have focus groups and the Beatles didn't use market research. However, it can take great courage to show up publicly with your most authentic work. It is often very tempting to edit, adapt and even hide out. But, believe me, there are people out there who will enjoy and *love* your most authentic work.

To be truly successful and authentic at doing what you love, you will need to access the deeper core that lies beyond your exterior personality. This means centring yourself in a place other than your mind and character. Every creative and artistic person knows that the place from which we create authentically is not our personality, but a deeper self – our soul or deepest being. Your deeper self has not been programmed. It is still pristine, eternal, wise, ever present, shining and untouched by any of your life experiences.

I also think of this deeper self as being our 'professional core', as it is central to our ability to do the work we love. As we discover more and more ways in which to access our professional core, so we learn how to self-validate rather than ask others for approval. We don't fear rejection or failure so much, because they don't touch the core of us. To that core, our successes and failures are simply experiences, not definitions of our identity.

Accessing our professional core enables us to understand that we are greater than any success or failure we might ever experience. We enjoy appreciation and success, just as we learn lessons from criticism and failure, yet we know that there is part of us which is greater than and untouched by either praise or criticism. Similarly, we are not carried away by success. Instead, we know that success is simply the natural by-product of doing our work.

When you turn pro and learn to self-validate, be willing to collaborate with and learn from other pros. By doing so, you will find yourself in a place of greater trust in relation to both yourself and others. For example, you might get yourself coached and mentored to improve your performance, and you might hire the services of other pros who excel at the things you are not so good at. Just as you respect them and their work, so you will enjoy their respect for yours.

Section 5:

Being the Leader of Your Tribe

Business success comes from leadership – and one of the best ways to create a successful business today is to find a group of people whom you can help to get to where they want to go. This can mean serving a 'tribe', an invitation to lead yourself and others. It involves going to place that you are inspired by and then inspiring others to go there too, showing them what route to take.

There are people who want and need you and what you do

'The world is waiting for what you have to offer – but don't always expect it to be easy – people need you to be happy, aligned with yourself to shine your light and share your gift.'

Alexandra Watson
Author of The Happiness System for Women

(Before I begin, I would like to acknowledge Seth Godin, whose fascinating book, *Tribes*, has inspired much of my thinking in this section.)

Budding Inspired Entrepreneurs often ask me the following questions: 'But do people need what I am going to do? Is there a market out there for me? Does the world need another writer/coach/children's party organiser/ healer/management consultant?' These are valid points to raise, and I think the answer has several layers to it.

Firstly, it's not about being just *another* coach, poet, artist or consultant. That sort of definition implies reducing yourself to a mere function. The question comes back to whether the work represents your true calling and purpose in life. If it is in your heart to do the work, then your work is destined to be received by and treasured by somebody out there. Your calling and your gifts are community property: what you love doing will be a blessing to someone. You are a unique part of creation and have been imagined and created for a particular purpose – to inhabit a special corner in creation that is completely yours. No one else has the special combination of insights, experience and understanding that you do. When you show up authentically, you will be the answer to somebody's prayers.

So my answer is this: the more you fully inhabit your own individuality and become your authentic self, then – yes – you will find the people out there for whom you are the right person.

Another way of looking at it is that you and your work will not be right for everyone; but you aren't supposed to be and never could be, so don't try. It can be tempting to think, 'How can I create an audience for my work? Who do *they* want me to be?' However, I would encourage you to have faith that an audience already exists for whatever it is in your heart to do. Sometimes that audience shows up immediately, but it may only appear over time. And it is most likely to emerge when you are simply yourself, rather than when you have moulded yourself into some version of what you think you ought to be.

Seth Godin is a great writer on digital marketing and trends, and in his book *Tribes* he argues that the world is increasingly coalescing around specific interest groups, causes, passions and subjects – i.e. forming tribes. And I believe that this is true.

When you create the work you love to do, it is highly unlikely to be a mass-market offering and I doubt you'd even want it to be. Today, you can build a successful business by serving a few dozen or few hundred clients who really like you, trust you, and enjoy the way you operate and do business. Your job is to become clear about who you are, what you stand for, what you can help with, and then go find the people who need your help, inspiration, education, support or entertainment. Then you will become the leader of a tribe of your own, putting yourself in the service of your tribal members, helping them get to where they want to go. Your tribe can be defined by geography, shared values, age, experience, interests – today it is possible to run a global business from your back bedroom.

It's reassuring to think of this way: instead of trying to persuade six billion people to do business with you, be curious and creative about how you can find the right fifty, hundred or two hundred people for whom you'll be a great fit and who will be grateful to you for what you do.

Build your tribe

'Your success is driven in large part by your ability to leverage the community you build around you.'

David Teten and Scott Allen
Authors of The Virtual Handshake

It can be reassuring to know your job is not to get everyone out there to like what you do in your work and business. There will be some people for whom you and your work resonate, and many – probably many more – for whom it won't. Don't take this personally as it's just how it's supposed to be. Not everyone is destined to be your client – although for some people you and the work you love to do will be the ideal solution, even the answer to their prayers.

Let me offer you the idea of 'natural monopoly', which means knowing that you and your work will be the end of the search for some people; they'll be happy with you and will call off their quest to find someone else who fits the bill. They will get to know you, like you, trust you and may then hire you or buy from you. The world is full of hype, noise and sales pitches, but most people just want to find someone whom they can trust and rely upon. So, be trustworthy, be open, be honest, be authentic and real. Show up in your work and get yourself seen by those people for whom you could be a great fit. Get yourself out there and known, so that you can attract more and more clients, and serve them beautifully. Your followers and advocates are your gold – they are precious and the lifeblood of your business.

Even if you start with just a single client or advocate, they are a demonstration of your success.

One of the challenges for many Inspired Entrepreneurs is that they can become too focused on doing what they love, and then fail to package what they do in a way which will meet clients' and customers' expectations or help solve their problems. At one end of the spectrum, it's possible to lose ourselves in the work we love to the extent that we become self-absorbed and self-indulgent; whereas at the other end of the spectrum are the conventional entrepreneurs, who sell out and only do whatever will make them a buck. So aim to find the sweet intersection of your own passions, talents and joy with what the world really needs and wants. Therein lies your vocation, the place where you can build your tribe and create openings to success.

Start thinking about 'building a tribe', rather than trying to sell and market yourself to the masses. You will create a niche, but grow that niche and you can have a successful business. When you find one client for whom you are a great fit (but not someone who is a friend or family member – they don't count, they're just being nice to you!), then you have already started to build your tribe. You may only need a few dozen people in your tribe, and as you do a good job with them, they will spread the word for you. Their good will could become your best marketing tool.

These days, it is less likely that you will need to build your tribe by 'broadcasting' messages impersonally at them, as has traditionally been the case in the conventional media. The old model meant interrupting people with adverts as they watched TV, listened to the radio or read papers and magazines, and in effect shouting: 'I'm here and I'm great, so please buy my product or service!' Today, with blogs, websites and social media, the way to build your tribe is to engage personally with people. Join in conversations over the Internet, share ideas, build relationships, share some of your expertise and then some of those people will become either your clients or your advocates. That is the way business is going: relationship first and then business follows from relationship. Know you, like you, trust you, experience you and then become your client...

Show up – be willing to be seen and known

'You have a responsibility to market your business and share your gifts.'

Michael Port
Author of Book Yourself Solid

Employment thinking often goes along these lines: we'll succeed by sticking to the rules; we shouldn't do too much without prior approval; and we should avoid risks so we won't fail or be stuck with any blame. But whilst that way of thinking may have brought us some security in our jobs, it is not actually a good strategy for success in our own businesses.

In my twenty years of giving talks and workshops, I have found that, when asked, most people acknowledge that their main area of weakness is not their talent, competence, expertise, knowledge or wisdom. It is that they are unknown, anonymous and largely invisible to the people they could serve and who might like to hire them.

Are you willing to give up being unknown and anonymous? Think about it for a moment. You have talents and gifts that could enhance the lives of others. You know you have. What if the people who need what you have to offer never have their lives enriched by you, because you never showed up –meaning they couldn't find you? They lose, you lose. So don't be selfish. Let other people know about you. As we saw in Section 2, showing up is very different from showing off. Showing off is saying, 'Look at me.' Showing up is a very generous act, and it's the magical process which enables a match to be made – it means that whoever needs you can find you, and vice-versa.

We have already talked about brilliance. Your brilliance is less effective if too few people experience it or know about it. You need to be seen and known. Hiding out and waiting to be discovered are not usually successful business strategies. But this doesn't mean you have to become an obnoxious self-promoter, who tries to turn everyone you know into a potential customer. What it does mean is this:

- People need to know that you exist and what kind of person you are. You need to show up authentically as yourself.
- There has to be something that they can call on you for – what can you help them with? What problems can you help them solve or what results can you help them achieve?
- What are your offerings? How do you package your services or products so that they can start engaging with you?

Demonstrate your skills, experience and wisdom by becoming a contributor, by giving and sharing. This is not a route to overnight success, but it is the route to building a solid and reliable business in time. When people know you, like you and trust you, they can either enter into a conversation about how you could help them, or they can start becoming advocates for you: they can rave to others about you.

Becoming visible can often entail both fear and excitement. It is exciting to show up, be seen and become known, yet at the same time we fear judgement, criticism, looking stupid, or feeling inadequate. Acknowledge that it will probably be a journey for you. So start small. Show up in small ways: perhaps write a blog post or create an article. Then maybe create some audio. Then a video. Then maybe a talk. Then try affiliating with others. Take a step, face a fear and grow in confidence – and then take another step. When you show up authentically rather than in some modified form, you will create connections and make a ripple. You will attract positive attention and interest. And you will find clients. The act of showing up and the way in which you show up are both crucial to your success.

By showing up, you can lead your tribe

'Generous and authentic leadership will always defeat the selfish efforts of someone doing it can because she can.'

Seth Godin
Author of Tribes

Becoming the initiating force in your own life and moving from a job or career into your own business is, to my mind, an act of leadership. Leadership is about causing transformation and making things better – for yourself and for others. It's about being an initiator rather than waiting for others to take the lead. When we initiate change and take charge of our lives, we bring out more of our talents and gifts; and the world is all the better for it. Leadership is about creating positive change.

However, today more than ever, leadership doesn't need to be about holding pole position. We can all be leaders in our own lives and by helping others be happier. Today, leadership is simply a matter of choice. True leadership is purely about being a friend to the world.

I think the core qualities of leadership are caring and character. I also believe that generosity is at the heart of authentic leadership. To truly lead we must truly care, not just use our position as a marketing stunt. As we learn to live in harmony with the guidance of our hearts, each choice we make becomes another way of telling our story, gathering our tribe, and liberating not only our own heart but the hearts of others. So the greatest way to build a business is to put ourselves in the service of our clients. This doesn't mean becoming a doormat or a martyr, but truly getting to know how we can help and serve our clients. Be as clear as you can about what you really care about and then let other people know about it. Inspired Entrepreneurs succeed because they care about people and are willing to help people get to where they want to get to.

Authentic leadership is actually quite simple:

- Do what inspires you and what you believe in and care about.
- Paint a picture of the future that inspires you and others, and that people want to get to.
- Go there yourself so that you are a living example.
- Inspire others to its possibility and map the route for people to follow: teach them 'how' and walk with them.

Leadership isn't complicated, but we have mostly been trained to avoid it; to avoid putting ourselves in a place of visibility so we won't be in the firing line or become targets for criticism or attack. The upside is that leading first yourself, and then leading others to where they want to go, can be the best job in the world. It is hugely fulfilling as it allows us to learn, grow and become pioneers, then share all we've learned in order to enhance the lives of others. It is an honour to truly serve people through your business and it is an incredible privilege when people follow and trust you.

You don't need any particular credentials, to be either anointed or appointed, to lead; you just need to care and to be willing to inspire, support and teach others. And it will be uncomfortable at times; for instance, standing up in front of strangers, proposing ideas that might fail, allowing yourself to be seen and known. But if you are not uncomfortable in your work as a leader, it's almost certain you are not reaching your full potential as one. Be willing to become more comfortable with your discomfort, as it shows you are growing.

Building your leadership platform

'I became successful because I was willing to give up being anonymous.'

Sophia Lauren
Actress

Our platform enables us to be seen and become known in the world; it helps us to build our tribes – to connect with the people who are or who could be interested in becoming our clients. Technologically, it has never been easier to create a platform for yourself for very little money – or even for free. You don't have to love technology, but love what technology can do to support your creativity, get your voice out there and help you serve more people more easily.

Here are the four major strategies I have used to get myself seen and known and to build my platform over the last twenty years:

1. *Networking – live and online:* meet people on a one-to-one basis and engage them in interesting conversations.

2. *Speaking*: give talks to your target audience. Contribute to their own ideas and growth, and share your experiences.

3. *Writing and publishing:* share ideas, information and expertise through writing articles, blogs, tips sheets,

books, e-books. Today, this can easily extend to
publishing audio and video on your blog and web site.

4. *Affiliating and joint venturing:* join forces with those
   who already have access to the people you'd like to
   be in front of, and get them to endorse you to their
   audience.

One of my most successful strategies has been to create
very valuable programmes, which I then give away for
free. This has helped me to create an email database
of over 20,000 people, and then build networks on
Facebook, Twitter and Linkedin. It is counterintuitive
in some ways, but giving away some of my best work
has been the best thing I have ever done to create a
successful business.

Your platform is comprised of your website, blog, free
programmes, audio and videos, articles, tip sheets –
everything and anything which helps you establish your
credibility in the eyes of others.

Other elements of a platform may include:

- Newspaper or magazine columns.
- An Internet presence, including a website or blog.
- Online social media presence (e.g., Facebook,
  Twitter, Digg and other social sites).
- Mailing lists (online and/or offline).
- Media exposure through your own television or
  radio programme, a recurring segment on a show or
  frequent guest appearances on a variety of shows.
- A high-profile job or political position.
- Prominence in professional organisations
  (e.g., as a board member).

Although you do not have to have all of these things to create an effective platform, the more visibility you enjoy the better. Start small and build.

One fear you may have is that, by becoming more visible, you will attract criticism. Don't shy away from this. You will probably have to learn cope with critics, but don't hide out in an attempt to avoid them – indeed, I suggest you actively welcome criticism. Criticism means that you are making an impact; that you are becoming known and that people are paying you attention. My personal experience is that ninety-nine per cent of the attention you are likely to attract will be positive (unless you are deliberately setting out to be controversial!), and any small amount of judgement or criticism is far outweighed by the joys and benefits of your being known.

Tell your own authentic story

'Marketing is the act of telling stories about the things we make – stories that sell and spread… today, marketing is about engaging with the tribe and delivering products and stories that spread.'

Seth Godin
Author of Tribes

To be persuaded to follow and trust you, people will want to know more about you and your own journey, and what has brought you to be doing what you do and offering what you offer.

So why are you doing what you do? What is your sense of purpose? Have you always done it? If not, what were you doing before? Why did you change? What obstacles have you had to overcome? What is your greatest joy from doing this new work? What keeps you passionate about it? What are your vulnerabilities? What do you struggle with? What pain do you help heal?

I visit many websites that convey very well what people do and how they do it, but I rarely come away from them with a strong sense of *why* people are doing what they do. I think people today will be hungry to get a sense of the purpose behind why you do what you do. So make it personal. Explain why. Tell your authentic story as it will engage and inspire people, and create an emotional bond with them. However, this will mean revealing your heart, your emotions. It may also disengage some people, but that might be all to the good as they might not be the right clients for you. Be bold and you will create strong connections with 'your people' instead.

Whether they are aware of it or not, I think people will be seeking answers to three big questions when they meet you, visit your blog or website, and those questions, which may lead to further related questions, are:

1. *How you can help them?* What is your field of expertise? What problems do you help people solve and what results do you help them achieve?

2. *Why you do this work?* Why do you love it? What is your own story and where does your credibility come from? What is your sense of purpose?

3. *What are your deliverables?* What can people buy from you? Do you have a free programme so that they can sample you at low risk and try you out?

If you find convincing answers to these three areas, then you will truly convey a sense of yourself and your work, and engage people effectively.

Build networks of people who look forward to hearing from you

'Selling to people who actually want to hear from you is more effective than interrupting strangers who don't.'

Seth Godin
Author of Tribes

One of your goals needs to be to build what are called 'permission assets'. That sounds very technical, but in essence what it means is this: the greatest asset you can create is a network of people who are willing to hear from you and who actually want to hear from you. Permission assets are an integral part of Permission Marketing: this is when people give you their permission to stay in touch with them and you therefore communicate regularly with them. It is a path towards building your business. When you are known, liked, trusted, and people anticipate and look forward to hearing from you, you will have put yourself in a strong place. We live in an attention economy – there are so many people wanting and competing for our attention. When people willingly give us their attention, it is a great gift and blessing.

What does this look like in practice? It looks like a database of physical addresses, or email addresses, or a network of friends on Facebook, or followers on Twitter. People who willingly give you their attention. It's not just about numbers; more importantly, it's about trust, quality and depth of connection you have with people.

The traditional business world has taught us how to create tasks and transactions, but business today is also about being social and sociable, about supporting friends and colleagues in useful and meaningful ways. When we become known as genuine contributors, we create what is called 'social capital', which in essence is our reputation, what people think of us in the social world and what they say about us rather than what we say about ourselves. Paradoxically, if we don't set out to build social capital, but set out instead to become a valuable resource in people's lives – to be contributors – we will build social capital as a by-product. Today, what other people say about you is becoming even more important than what you say about yourself.

Technology enables us to connect with more people more easily than ever before in history, but remember that people's attention is a precious and valuable resource, so don't squander it. Treasure it and use it wisely, as they have a lot of other options when it comes to demands on their time and interest. Always use technology to serve, uplift and inspire, rather than to create a lot of noise simply to draw attention to yourself. Turn strangers into friends and friends into customers. The Internet is increasingly about connections rather than transactions. As we discussed earlier, your greatest possibility for success comes from friendship first and then some of those friends will become clients.

Understand the power of 'authentic niching'

'We are all experts in our own little niches.'
Alex Trebek
Game show host

It can feel luxurious to wallow in the belief that 'anyone could be my customer. So many people could need what I do.' But, as we have seen, the truth is that not everyone will be your client. There will be some people with whom you resonate more than others, who will feel drawn to you, like you and trust you. And others won't. So don't try to be everything to everybody – that's a recipe for ineffectiveness and stress. Instead, become significant, a valuable source and resource for a small group of people. Serve them well and they will bring others to you. Learn how to make a particular group yearn for what you can do for them. Rather than setting manipulative traps to capture them, create a honey-pot that they will love returning to as they desire the new world you can give them. Remember that today we trust what our friends tell us much more than we trust advertising or what companies tell us about themselves.

Your own authentic niche will flow from your calling, and is often born out of the obstacles you have experienced and overcome, the results you have achieved, and your experiences and expertise. So many businesses are born out of a particular problem that somebody has experienced and solved, realising in the process that lots of other people have the same or a similar problem. For example, Sarah Tremellen, the co-founder of Bravissimo (a firm that supplies lingerie for fuller-figured women), started her business in her living room in 1997 with a friend. She said: 'When I became pregnant, I went up several bra sizes and couldn't get any pretty bras in my size. I remember being shown larger cups in some dark corner of the store. I had always wanted to set up a business and liked the idea of doing something that would make a difference. As well as produce a good range of bras, it's all about women celebrating their curves.' She began by sending an email to a list of seventy of her friends and family. That first mailing generated just four orders, but she saw that there was interest and soon she'd created a buzz around her range. Bravissimo – the company she co-owns with her husband Mike – employs 650 people and recorded a turnover of £44.4million in 2009.

The more you create a micro-niche around your unique calling, the more powerful you will become. Chrissie Slade came on a course of mine called 'Creating Your Expert Brand' and has since created her own authentic niche. Chrissie is now a – if not *the* – expert on aromatherapy for guinea pigs! She has a passion for guinea pigs, and developed a range of oils suited to them. She now supplies products all over the world. It's a pretty narrow niche, but by focusing that sharply, she has built a successful business around her passion, interest and skills.

Focused niches that you love and serve well can spawn fabulous businesses. There is power in authentic niching, as it will help you to develop real expertise.

Section 6:

Being Enough

Ironically, the experience of starting and running your own business, doing the work you love and serving others, is likely to feed any beliefs or feelings you may have of not being good enough or not being up to the job in hand. It is also, however, an invitation to discover greater resources and powers within yourself, and to explore your own significance, worth and impact. It is an invitation to great self-love. You already have an adequate and successful self within you, and you can learn to access and live from that core.

Your successful self

'Success is about recognising the self you came to earth with, and whilst success can add to happiness, happiness is more likely to help you be successful.'

Dr Robert Holden
Author of Success Intelligence

One of the most insidious and corrosive forms of resistance that the majority of us will experience is simply this: we don't believe we are enough. In various and often subtle ways, we feel lacking, inadequate, overwhelmed; we doubt and we undermine ourselves – at least I do! The journey of starting and running our own business is also a journey into discovering our own adequacy, into our natural talents, into simply *being enough*, defying and denying the voices which doubt our potential – and having the courage to start our business anyway.

It can be tempting to succumb to the belief that some magical day exists in the future, when the circumstances of your life will grant you the freedom you crave and you will feel ready and up to the adventure that lies ahead. But as the writer Sheldon Kopp expressed it so well: 'I have never embarked upon a journey for which I felt adequately prepared.' So don't be tempted to wait until you feel confident and adequate; you will become confident and feel adequate by having the courage to start anyway. Your confidence and ability will show up when you do. I love the words of the Trappist monk Thomas Merton, who said: 'Do it trembling if you must, but do it.'

There already is a successful self within you – the inner self with which you arrived here on earth, and which is pristine, innately intelligent and creative. This inner self is whole and strong enough to face all the opportunities and challenges you will meet during your life, yet it is unaffected by your experiences in this world. In this respect it is very akin to your professional core, with which it is inextricably linked (see Section 4). It is contains wonderful resources, talents and abilities, but is blessedly free from stories about why you can't succeed. This self has nothing to prove, but simply wants to be itself. In my favourite spiritual text, *A Course in Miracles*, this part of us is called our 'grandeur'; it relates to how we were created, and is pretty amazing. There is grandeur in everyone. I call this our 'unconditional self'.

But there is yet another self within you, and that is a self which has learned its ideas about itself based on what you have been told by your parents, teachers, employers and all the other influences you have had in your life. This self knows many stories, beliefs, ideas and attitudes, but these usually relate to what it can't do and what its limits are. This is your 'conditioned self'. Whilst you are truly an unlimited being, you probably live with a very limited sense of yourself. You know in your heart that you are capable of greatness; that there is grandeur within you. But it can be as scary as it is exciting to venture outside the limits imposed by your conditioned self.

In my experience, when we get a sense of our inner grandeur or unconditional self, we may well wonder whether we are getting too big for our boots. In 1986, when I seriously began to contemplate giving up my job selling computers to Japanese banks to start a more purposeful way of life, running my own business as a speaker, trainer, writer and life coach, I judged myself very harshly. I would ask myself, 'Who do I think I am? I'm just a computer salesman from Hornchurch, who can't even keep myself inspired for more than five minutes – who'll ever listen to me or take me seriously?' I am sure you recognise that sort of internal dialogue. Your unconditional self is always reminding you of what you can become, and the unrealised potential you have within you.

I have been on a 'personal growth journey' since 1986. What does that mean to me? In essence, it has meant excavating the unconditional self that is already within me and then developing a personality which works with and supports my success, rather than judges it and tries to undermine it. To me, that is daily work.

My challenge to you is this: are you willing to act courageously on your inner calling right now – in anticipation of feeling good enough and adequate enough in the future?

Your own heroic journey

'A hero is someone who has given his or her life to something bigger than oneself.'

Joseph Campbell
Mythologist

Creating, running and building your business is your own heroic journey. It takes courage to heed that inner call. It takes courage to believe in your own intrinsic value, your significance, your gifts and talents; that you are needed and wanted in this world.

We tend to do think of heroes as needing villains to triumph over, but being an Inspired Entrepreneur is a different form of heroism. As Inspired Entrepreneurs, our heroic quest is about saying 'yes' to our precious unconditional self and, in so doing, becoming more fully alive and more effective in this world. The real things to triumph over are our own fears, our own dragons and demons so that we can reach the self-in-potential that is already within us – our unconditional self. The task of releasing that treasure is part of the Universe's grand plan and destiny for each of us, and the answer as to why we were put on this planet. In every decision there is a choice between love and fear, but we can make new decisions in each moment.

In this respect, there are two journeys you are embarking upon in your quest to do the work you love:

1. *The creation of visible, tangible results around your business for the world to see.* This means your products, services, websites and brochures; your

money in the bank; your clients and customers;
the impact you have and the ripples you cause; the
feedback you get and the contribution you make;
the hearts you touch.

2.   *The invisible and heroic journey that you go through
     to make things visible in the world.* This involves
     your own personal inner journey, which most
     people will never witness and which many wouldn't
     necessarily understand. It's the choices you make;
     the courage you have had to find; the insights and
     intelligence you gain along the way; the practice
     and the obstacles you have to overcome.

As your inner journey is only fully seen and experienced
by you, you'll need to learn to honour and appreciate
yourself, to give yourself 'positive strokes' (see Section 7,
'Create your own life-affirming structures'), and to self-
validate. You can learn to affirm your self-worth if you
don't feel it is affirmed by others. It is wonderful when
you find other people who are willing to honour you,
mentor you, encourage you, see your potential and share
a sense of your own journey, but ultimately it can be
nobody else's job but yours to love and honour yourself,
to be your own best friend and ally.

When I researched my first book, *The Work We Were
Born to Do*, I discovered that by the time most of us
reach adulthood we will have received about nine times
as many negative messages about ourselves as positive
ones. The ration is about 225,000 to 25,000. That
seemed to make sense to me and helped me understand
my own low self-esteem. If you resonate with this,
you may find it hard to believe in yourself, appreciate
yourself or be kind to yourself. Learning to love yourself
will be an important part of your own heroic journey.

You will also need to do your best to give up comparing yourself and your progress with others, as you will probably only end up feeling bad about yourself if you don't. Your journey is yours alone, while other people will have their own journeys to make. What you find excruciatingly difficult, others will find easy. On the other hand, what might be a breeze for you, others may struggle with for years. No one's journey is any greater or lesser than yours.

When you choose to follow the path to your most authentic and precious unconditional self, you will experience many ups and downs, triumphs and defeats, all of which are precisely what you need to help you shed unhelpful beliefs and blossom into your full potential. Learn to trust that whatever you experience contains a gift, however badly wrapped that present may be and however much it may at first look like trouble, difficulty or disappointment.

Living at your thresholds

'Think of yourself as on the threshold of unparalleled success. A whole, clear, glorious life lies before you. Achieve! Achieve!'

Andrew Carnegie (1835–1919)
Scottish–American industrialist, businessman,
entrepreneur and a major philanthropist

One of the great joys of being an Inspired Entrepreneur is that it puts us on an evolutionary path; our inspiration constantly draws us forward. It keeps taking us to new frontiers – places that bring us to life in greater ways and which call us to blossom into our full potential. Inspiration invites us into new conversations with ourselves, those around us and with our vocations.

As Inspired Entrepreneurs, we are pioneers in the outside world, doing the things we have not done before and putting ourselves in new situations; and also pioneers within ourselves, as we find new resources, skills and talents that have perhaps lain dormant within us thus far. Inspiration calls us to become more of ourselves. Like a tissue box, the more we discover of ourselves, the more we find there is to discover. We are all multilayered.

I find it often surprises Inspired Entrepreneurs when their passion and inspiration for what they do wane a little. Rather than admit it, they often try to work harder at what they are already doing. But life is about growth. We may have outgrown whatever it was that inspired us a year ago, but that doesn't mean our inspiration has completely gone; rather, it usually means that inspiration is inviting us to open a new chapter, to cross a new threshold. Often a slight waning of enthusiasm means we are called to graduate to something more positively challenging, which is a better fit for what we have become and a fuller expression of our gifts and qualities.

When you live regularly at thresholds, you remain more alive. A threshold is a place of anticipation and possibility. To cross new thresholds continuously during the course of your life requires both a willingness to listen inwardly, to hear the messages and ideas within yourself, and a willingness to be honest with yourself rather than dismissive about what you hear.

One of the easiest ways to identify where your next threshold might lie is simply to ask yourself questions such as:

- What would inspire you next in your work or business?
- What are the projects you are most resisting now?
- What is your soul calling you to next in your business?
- What fear are you currently facing?

…and to honestly want to listen to the answers.

Sometimes you may be called into new territory that at first seems too big and scary for you; but you are being invited to grow, embody new qualities, quit playing too small, and to express more of the true greatness and brilliance that is within you. Often, though, you may feel you lack the confidence you need to make the transition. And there can be an element of truth in that. But if you are willing to show up in new ways, a new sense of confidence will start to show up when you do. But you can't create confidence in theory, only by crossing thresholds. You will grow through action.

Learn to trust in what your deeper self guides you to do next.

Out of the shadows and into your brilliance

'The biggest curse on the world is your unlived life.'

Carl Jung (1875–1961)
Swiss psychiatristInfluential thinker and
founder of analytical psychology.

You may not feel that you are good enough because there remain qualities, gifts and talents that have yet to be drawn out of you. Sometimes the brilliance you need to succeed in your business can be found in the positive shadow of your life so far. Let me explain. A 'shadow interest' means an area of interest, passion and curiosity which you love and enjoy being around, but where you never put your own talent out there fully. For example, you may dream of writing a book, so you go to work in a branch of Waterstone's where you are surrounded by books, can buy books at discounts, get to meet people every day who love books and sometimes get to meet authors too. On one level your passion is being fed, but on another level it goes hungry: you are resisting and hiding out because you are not writing your own book.

Here are some other ways in which you may be living a shadow life:

- Supporting the talent of others, rather than acknowledging and developing your own talent.

- Being public and showing up, but for something that isn't close to your own heart and isn't authentically you.
- Beavering away on your creative projects in private, but never putting them out for public scrutiny.
- Playing safe with projects, rather than initiating the projects that feel most exciting and scary for you.
- Focusing on the mundane parts of your business rather than the cutting edge, where you'd really make a difference.
- Denying that you even have any talent of your own and always believing it is others who have talent.
- Believing that your identity and credibility originate from the kudos of working for a prestigious company rather than for yourself – and that you'd be nothing on your own.

Basically, you are probably hiding out, but you don't even realise it. The first stage is to become aware.

This happened for me in 1997, when I realised that being a director of Alternatives in London had become yet another way of hiding out for me. There I was, promoting the spirituality and creativity of others, while my own voice remained largely quiet. It had been fun meeting and working some world-class authors and speakers, but I was growing bored. I had things to say too, but I was afraid to say them, believing that others would and could say them much better than I could ever do. However, I realised that I didn't want to organise talks for others as much as I wanted to give talks myself.

All shadow artists are actually afraid to put their creativity at the centre of their own lives. We need to become honest with ourselves and say, 'You know what – I *am* terrified; I don't know if I'm that creative, if I have anything new to say or whether I can even do it. But I'm willing to find out...'

Inspiration calls us to move beyond our fear to the full expression of our creativity. The poet David Whyte reminds us: 'Life is constantly orphaning us from our old homes, but always into a much larger territory than we think we can inhabit to start with.' As the aphorism says, 'Sometimes even eagles need a push to leave their nests and fly.'

Coming out of the shadows is part of your journey as an Inspired Entrepreneur. Where might you be living a shadow life? Where is life calling you to show up more?

Integrate your shadow

'When our lives are not working, there is always at least one thing we're not facing, and looking away from what you need to face burns more energy than actually facing it.'

Gay Hendricks
Author of Conscious Living

The poet and mythologist Robert Bly has spoken about our shadow side in his work. He describes it as being all that we have decided wasn't acceptable about us. Bly suggests that at birth we arrive as 360 degrees of energy and vitality, but that as we grow up we are told, or surmise, that certain aspects of ourselves are not acceptable within our family, school, job or community. These qualities cannot be eradicated but can be lost to conscious access.

Robert Bly creates an image of a black bag into which we put our 'undesirable' qualities. So, at home we may put our anger in the bag; at school we put our exuberance and curiosity into the bag; whereas at work we put our initiative into it and just do as we are told. By the time we reach adulthood, a good quantity of our vitality may be in that bag. The bag represents our shadow, consisting of qualities that we have judged as 'bad,' but obviously many of our strengths end up in there too. Robert Bly suggests that this process is what we endure in order to become 'civilised', or as my friend Dr Chuck Spezzano calls it: 'God frozen people.' When we embark on any kind of growth, we are really starting on the path of taking qualities out of the bag little by little and integrating them back into our everyday lives. Indeed, we can spend the rest of our lives reclaiming ourselves.

In the household and school where I grew up, I decided that creativity was unwelcome, unimportant and of no value. So I threw my creativity into the bag. If anyone had asked me between the ages of twenty and thirty if I was at all creative, my answer would have been an unequivocal 'No!', but gradually I wondered whether there might be a shred of creativity in me. I started to create talks, then workshops, then I began to write. And I realised there was a lot of creativity in me. Six books, hundreds of articles and dozens of CDs and DVDs and online-learning programmes later, I realise there was and is a massive amount of creativity in me, but I needed to acknowledge, re-own and practise it because I had relegated it to my shadows when I was young.

I am sharing this for one reason: to make you aware that, in order to succeed in your business and in doing what you love, you may need more than the qualities you have currently have. You may well need to learn practical skills such as accounting, handling cash flow, building websites and social media, but you may also need to look into your own black bag and see what qualities may be there which you have denied or judged – and then start to bring them back into conscious use. Or you may find that qualities you thought you should only use outside work, such as authenticity or caring, are actually needed within your work for it to be successful.

This is why I think running your own business is such a fabulous opportunity to learn, grow and become who you are. The experience continually invites you to dig deep and discover more about yourself, your gifts, talents and qualities, so that you can become a whole and complete human being. Sometimes you may not initially like what you find, but the deeper you look, the greater the treasures you will discover. You may have learned to leave some of the best elements of your humanity outside the office door. But your own business calls you to unearth and reclaim the best qualities and gifts you have – to show up with them in your work as they will be the very key to your success.

The courage to face your vulnerability

'Your pain is the breaking of the shell that encloses your understanding. Even as the stone of the fruit must break, that its heart may stand in the sun, so must you know pain.'

Kahlil Gibran
Author of The Prophet

There will be times as an Inspired Entrepreneur when you are likely to feel vulnerable, which is not a word often used in work and business settings. But when you are pioneering across new thresholds in your life, you are indeed likely to feel vulnerable. And you may feel uncomfortable around that vulnerability. Where there is excitement and promise, there can equally be doubt and inadequacy. Old feelings can resurface. To live an authentic and vibrant life, you are going to need to make friends with vulnerability. Personally, I've found that the times of vulnerability which I've experienced were great blessings, helping to open me up, although when I was going through them they were painful and difficult.

A place of vulnerability can be a birthing place, where we shed some kind of skin – be it an old way of working, habitual behaviour, a way of being, relating or showing up. It's when whatever we once gave meaning to no longer feels authentic or relevant. Some other, more real part of us wants to emerge. But we often feel the death part rather than the birth part of the process and so resist letting go.

I think there are two paths we can follow:

1. *The path of defensiveness*: keeping our armour on and rarely letting ourselves be vulnerable so we can't be hurt or disappointed again. We tend to erect defences where we have experienced some pain or a wound, so it takes real courage to dismantle them.

2. *The path of gradually relinquishing our defences so that we can become more authentically ourselves.* This can sometimes feel like being broken open.

Through allowing ourselves to experience true vulnerability, we can start our own internal revolutions; we begin the return journey to our true selves rather than continue to live under the influence of our conditioned selves. In time, we may even give birth to the real self that has always been there.

In my experience, the most successful Inspired Entrepreneurs are willing to allow vulnerability into their lives. They know that it heralds a birthing place, a place of dying away and rebirth, of new life. At times this can be graceful. But they know it isn't always easy. Sometimes it is a quick process. Sometimes it is more like a dark night of the soul, with the fear that the dawn will never come again.

Our true potential is enormous, unlimited. But it must be made manifest through the prism of our personalities, which are formed of the multitude of small ideas we have about who we are and what we are capable of. Most of those ideas and beliefs are not even our own. They are what we have learned to believe about ourselves; they are our conditioned and inherited beliefs. We may have learned to regard our lives as some kind of compensation; the compensation is that we look good, but really we feel bad.

Your life running your own business will often involve your recognising, identifying and discarding those outdated old ideas about yourself, and embracing truer and more life-affirming beliefs about who you are, your real identity and all that you are capable of being.

As I have mentioned, it takes courage to be vulnerable. In my twenties I was very driven to be successful. As I began to slow down in my late twenties and early thirties, I began to see that deep down I actually felt a bit of a failure. And I was trying to use outer success as a means to escape from that sense of failure. But I couldn't run any more. No amount of outer success could help me feel what I didn't believe. I had to stop and look at those old beliefs and face some painful feelings. I raked through some of the conditioning surrounding my upbringing and I was able to come to some different decisions. But I felt very vulnerable. However, new and stronger ground began to emerge out of that process for me to stand on – I had a stronger sense of myself. I began to be more authentic, rather than feel I had to compensate and put on a good show. I began to become more real.

To face your own vulnerability, you may well need support from people who understand what it is like as they have faced their own vulnerabilities. Belief in something greater than yourself is also helpful, whether it is Life, your God, the Universe, a Higher Power. Knowing that there is a power within the Universe which supports you as you evolve into your greatest self is comforting – and I believe it's true. You may be familiar with the Kabbalistic tradition which says that every blade of grass has an angel looking over it, crying, 'Grow, evolve, become!' If a blade of grass is given this amount of love and support, imagine who might be on your invisible team, cheering and helping you to fulfil your potential!

Self-acceptance rather than self-improvement

'Always say "yes" to the present moment. What could be more futile, more insane, than to create inner resistance to something that already is? What could be more insane that to oppose life itself, which is now and always now?'

Eckhart Tolle
Author of The Power of Now

Another way to reach the point where we feel we are 'good enough' is through an ongoing process of self-acceptance. When I started out on my own journey of personal growth in 1985, I would say I was into what I would now call 'self-improvement'. The essence of this was that I told myself: 'There are some parts of me that I want to focus on and display to the world, and other parts of myself that I will do my best to eliminate or at least hide.' Another way of saying it would be: 'I want to focus on success and avoid failure – I want to focus on the light and avoid the dark.'

At the time, it seemed a very logical and sensible goal. But after about ten years, it began to dawn on me to my horror that my strategy wasn't working. I could still get angry and frustrated for Britain, still become depressed and despairing, all of which would plunge me into feeling an absolute failure and wanting to give up. I always ended up with this feeling that there must be something wrong with me.

Then I had the honour of meeting two spiritual teachers called Tom and Linda Carpenter in London. They lived in Hawaii, and invited my partner Helen and myself to go visit them if we wanted to. So we did. Visiting Kaui in Hawaii was magical. One evening, I was sitting on the deck at their home with Tom when he looked me in the eyes and said, 'There is nothing wrong with you.' I was blown away. It was one of those pivotal moments. Tom then went on to explain about deep self-acceptance as taught in *A Course in Miracles*. In that moment, I started along a new path in my life, work and business – the path of self-acceptance, which is really the path of self-love.

Self-love and self-leadership aren't about improving yourself, because there's nothing really wrong with you. It is more about remembering. Remembering your inner spirit and then making your relationship with it stronger each day. Self-leadership has a great deal to do with simply reconnecting with the person you once were – with your true nature.

Instead of trying to eliminate any challenging parts of myself, I now aim to love and accept those parts of me. I think that there are so many different parts inside all of us – some we like, and many that we may dislike and judge. Our job is to accept them all to the best of our abilities, and to manage the difficult parts so that we don't act them out or let them ruin our lives. The poet Rainer Maria Rilke said: 'Perhaps all the dragons of our lives are princesses who are only waiting to see us once, beautiful and brave. Perhaps everything terrible is in its deepest being something that needs our love.' By granting a certain degree of acceptance to whatever qualities we find hard to tolerate within ourselves, we become both freer and more potent. This means we can still love learning and growing for the rest of our lives, but from a place of greater fullness, rather than a place of inadequacy.

I recently heard an interview with Bruce Springsteen on a BBC Radio 2, in which he talked about song writing. When he was asked whether, at the age of fifty-seven with tens of millions of albums sold, he felt he was a success, he explained, 'Some parts of me feel a success, but there is no part of yourself that you can leave behind. You can only learn to manage the parts of yourself. It is like driving a car. There is a twelve-year-old, a twenty-two-year-old, a forty-year-old in there who has done pretty well, but there is also the guy who wants to drive the car into a tree and kill himself. That's never going to change. The doors are locked and sealed. But who is driving makes all the difference and the direction you are going. Nobody is going anywhere, it's a lifetime ride, but who is at the wheel makes the difference. You want the latest model of yourself that has sussed some of this stuff out and can drive you some place you want to go.' He understands that there are many parts of himself that he has to accept, live with and manage every day.

I would guess that, within you, there are elements that feel successful; parts of you that feel insecure and afraid; some parts of you which may want to sabotage your own efforts; parts of you that feel confident and inspired; and other parts that feel depressed, hopeless and powerless. There certainly are in me! So the question is less about, 'Why do we all have this menagerie inside us?' and rather, 'Who is that the wheel of your life today?' The good news is that you can decide who is at your wheel and which direction you are headed.

So who is in charge of your life today? What direction are you headed today?

Reinvention and many lives in this lifetime

'The professional does not permit himself to become hidebound within one incarnation, however comfortable or successful. Like a transmigrating soul, he shucks his outworn body and dons a new one. He continues his journey.'

Steven Pressfield
Author of The War of Art

True reinvention is not about waking up one day and deciding who you are going to be. It is about following the guidance of your Muse to go deeper into yourself and to connect more closely with your most authentic creative self at this particular point in your life. I suspect that during the course of your entrepreneurial career you will go through many reinventions, but each one will be truer expression of who you are at that point in your life. You will learn, you will mature; your defences will be challenged and ground down.

The direction of your re-inventions and reincarnations should always be towards greater authenticity. The reinvention of your daily life means marching off the edge of your maps and into new territory that you feel called to explore and inhabit.

Section 7:

Being a Kind Boss to Yourself

Being your own boss is a fantastic invitation to find freedom and to realise your own potential. But it can also be an invitation to be hard on yourself, to overwork and never feel like you are doing enough. You need to learn to become a kind, supportive and inspiring boss to yourself, encouraging yourself to your greatest success and celebrating yourself and your achievements along the way.

Becoming a great boss to yourself

'Genuine kindness is not what we do. It is what we are.'

Vernon Howard (1918–1992)
Author of Psycho-Pictography

I recently sent out a message on Twitter that said: 'I love working for myself, but the boss is often a bit demanding!' Loads of people responded that they frequently felt the same way. They loved the freedom of doing the work they love and running their own business, but they acknowledged that it is possible to overwork and set the bar too high too often. Running our own businesses can be an opportunity to be hard on ourselves, to criticise ourselves, always focusing on our weaknesses and forgetting to celebrate our victories, successes, growth and accomplishments. In short, it is important to remember to be kind to yourself, support yourself, celebrate yourself.

Whilst your business may allow you to enhance the lives of others – even express love and kindness for others – it is equally important that your business should also be a way of learning to love and be kind to yourself. It can be a vehicle for self-love too. May I suggest that one of your goals as an Inspired Entrepreneur is to answer these questions: how kind, loving, encouraging and supportive can you be to yourself? How wise and intelligent can you be in unleashing your own potential? How great a boss can you be to yourself? How much of a connoisseur of your own talent can you become?

It is a myth that success comes only as the result of hard work, struggle and sacrifice. Rather, it comes from finding and releasing the best of ourselves. So, how good a friend can you be to yourself? To what extent can you gain a positive sovereignty over your inner world? This will partly happen naturally if you are kind to yourself, but it can also become a conscious focus of how you operate. I suggest checking in with yourself regularly, and asking yourself, 'As a boss, how much do I enjoy working for myself? Would I encourage others to work with me and for me – or would I warn them off?'

Create your own life-affirming structures

'Through structure comes the greatest freedom.'
Rev Darrell W Boswell
Author of Building Better Churches

Inspired Entrepreneurs know that they need to support themselves by creating positive and life-affirming structures for themselves. Most will have been employed before starting their own business, so creating a structure for their new work may be pioneering territory for them. They realise that, just because they have left behind a structured environment, they are not necessarily free. True freedom depends on our attitude and how we structure our own lives. It's a myth that freedom is the absence of controlling or restrictive structures. Escaping control is not the same as creating autonomy.

Two of the most important human needs are structure and strokes. 'Structure' refers to our need to fit in, belong, have goals, plans and boundaries. 'Strokes' are units of social recognition – the human interaction, teamwork, the positive and negative feedback that we get from working with others.

If we are employed, we often dislike our work because it is over-structured and we crave greater freedom over our own time and goals. But to succeed and to be happy and healthy emotionally and spiritually, we still need structure. I would therefore suggest that you help nurture your own success by putting in place supportive and life-enhancing structures in your work.

This means that you will have to be honest and acknowledge the benefits that working for someone else can sometimes give us: structure and strokes. The loss of both of these can initially be extremely significant, yet unfortunately often remains unacknowledged when we start our own business. Sometimes this loss alone can cause people to go back to their old jobs before they have even reached the point in their new work where they are able to build a sense of structure or strokes back in, and thereby create a new sense of identity for themselves. It certainly took me years of running my own business before I could stop talking about what I used to do or who I used to work for.

So, as an Inspired Entrepreneur, you will need to create a plan of action for building structure and strokes back into the business you were born to create. However, if you have been employed for much of your life, another obstacle for you may be this: you may have become institutionalised to some extent. You may be used to having other people create structure for you by telling you where you fit in, what your goals need to be and what you should be doing and when. If this is the case, you will need to do two major things:

1. Give yourself permission to establish what your personal dreams, goals and ambitions are, and then give yourself permission to reach for those goals.

2. Create a clear structure in your work which enables you to take positive action and reach your own dreams and goals.

There is myth which says, 'Doing your own thing means doing it all alone.' This attitude can be a recipe for loneliness, leaving us feeling unsupported, unaccountable, without encouragement and ultimately destined for failure.

But there are very clear steps you can take to create structure in your life as an Inspired Entrepreneur:

- Establish coaching and mentoring relationships – whether paid or unpaid, or co-coaching relationships.
- Join inspiring networks, such as the Inspired Entrepreneur Community in London, where you can enjoy the fellowship of kindred spirits and feel you belong (see Appendix).
- Make friends with fellow Inspired Entrepreneurs by having lunch or coffee with them, supporting each other and holding each other accountable.
- Identify your own goals, create action plans and steps – and stick to these.
- Ensure you invest in continuing education and development for yourself through reading, attending talks, listening to audio and seminars.
- Find ways of taking stock, appraising your own successes, celebrating them; look at areas that didn't work so well and take the learning points from them.
- Join or create some kind of mastermind group, in which you can take part in brainstorming, get feedback and share accountability for what you are doing.

When we work alone, it is often easy to slide into believing that we are the only ones to have particular problems or situations, when in fact we are probably only going through what most other people experience. But it helps if we understand that our challenges are not the result of any character defect on our part, but simply part of the territory that goes with being an Inspired Entrepreneur. If you find yourself undergoing difficulties, rest assured that there is nothing wrong with you and that most people face similar challenges. An awareness of this will help you remain free to forge your own path, whilst at the same time benefiting from the wisdom and experience of others who are also forging their own paths. It can save a huge amount of time and heartache.

Understand that your identity will change and evolve as you work for yourself

'The purpose of life is for the individual to become greater than the definitions he has inherited.'

James Baldwin (1927–1987)
American writer and civil rights activist

One of the strongest forces in life is our need to live consistently within the boundaries created by a clear sense of identity – to know who we believe we are. But as the wonderful quotation above expresses, part of our life's journey is the evolution of our sense of identity and our understanding of who we are. As you embark on running your own business, you will find yourself bumping up against your own sense of limitation and also your conflicting desire to move beyond those limitations into a greater sense of yourself. This is a courageous journey, in my experience.

As you make the transition from being employed to self-employed, your sense of identity may change a lot. You may even have a temporary identity crisis, as you are no longer who you were and are not yet who you will become. However, an identity crisis can be a marvellous opportunity to trade in a limiting self-image for a greater and truer one. Your true identity is an amazing spirit, an incredible soul.

Nevertheless, when first starting up the business you were born to create, you may lose confidence and suffer from the lack of recognition, appraisal, feedback, training and support that often comes from working alongside others as an employee. This can be painful enough to make you want to return to the old structure you once knew. You may need to sit in a place of discomfort for a while as your old identity fades away and a new one begins to emerge. There can be some grief as well, which often catches people out. They make a conscious positive and life-affirming decision to do their own thing, but they didn't anticipate the sense of loss involved. This is natural and normal while you are in a stage of metamorphosis.

Your journey as an Inspired Entrepreneur will be one in which there is a continual dying away of limiting ideas about yourself and the continual revelation of a new sense of yourself, new possibilities and a new appreciation of the ways that you and your work can be received.

You are the leader of your business as well as the boss

'Leaders are not paid to be busy but to exercise quality thinking.'

Dr Robert Holden
Author of Success Intelligence

Your success will come from investing a lot of energy into your projects – but this needn't be just about hard work. Hard work alone will not bring you success; in fact, having hard work as your major strategy is very likely to be counter-productive and a block to your success. It doesn't have to involve struggle and sacrifice, pain and fear. Success will come from your love and creativity, joy and inspiration, clear and quality thinking, and courageous actions.

It is very possible to mistake busyness for effectiveness, and to trick yourself into thinking that merely because you are busy you are on track. Strategic and focused action is much more likely to bring you success than simply keeping yourself busy for the sake of it. At times, it can take courage to slow down and not give into the urge to push ourselves harder and harder.

When we take time out to think creatively, we will open ourselves up to the process of conceiving ideas and developing them into products, programmes or services – tangibles which we can deliver and from which we can earn money. Often, though, once we have created something and it is running well, we may become a bit bored and feel the urge to create something new. We all want to evolve. We therefore need to find constructive ways to keep ourselves engaged creatively, developing ourselves and our business, whilst also maintaining and generating more income.

As an Inspired Entrepreneur, you will need to think along several timescales:

- What you are delivering right now that earns you money?
- What you are in the process of developing? What marketing ideas, product ideas, systems ideas etc do you aim to implement in the next twelve months?
- What other new ideas and possibilities are you conceiving? How can you develop new projects which will come into being beyond the next twelve months?

When it comes to the business you were born to create, you are Director of Delivery, Development and Innovation, and you'll need to keep thinking about all three. This is what so many people love about their own business – that are they engaged in many ways and that they get to utilise so many of their different talents and abilities. You too were made to think brilliantly and see through the eyes of possibility, rather than think badly and see through the eyes of fear.

Work in and on your business

'If they don't fail outright, most businesses fail to fully achieve their potential. That's because the person who owns the business doesn't truly know how to build a company that works without him or her, which is the key.'

Michael Gerber
Author of The E-Myth Revisited

To create sustainable success, and to stay in love with your work and with running your business, you will need to understand a key distinction: the difference between working *in* your business and *on* your business.

I have been running my own business, doing what I love, for twenty years now, and these days I love what I do more than ever. But there have been times when I have nearly burned out and been close to falling out of love with my work. The major reason was that I was always working *in* my business – coaching over long hours, travelling to give talks and workshops to anyone and everyone who invited me, often for not much money, until gradually I became exhausted. I felt guilty if I wasn't working hard. I was still in the grip of the old Protestant work ethic, making myself suffer to justify my existence and success. I hadn't fully learned about the crucial importance of a couple of things:

1. Working *on* my business and not just *in* my business.

2. That I could embrace a work ethic based on inspiration and following my joy – and still be successful.

I first heard about the idea of working *on* a business as opposed to working *in* a business from Michael Gerber in his book, *The E Myth Revisited,* in 2000. Today, I probably spend as much time working on my business as I do in my business. Working in my business means giving talks, coaching, running workshops, organising events, meetings, admin and writing. Working on my business involves thinking, planning, developing, learning, growing, networking, being coached myself and switching off completely. Today, my mantra is this: there are lots of things I love doing, but none of them would I want to do every day.

Eight ways to work on your business, not just in your business

'Whatever results you're getting, be they rich or poor, good or bad, positive or negative, always remember that your outer world is simply a reflection of your inner world. If things aren't going well in your outer life, it's because things aren't going well in your inner life. It's that simple.'

T. Harv Eker
Author and seminar leader

Whilst 'working on your business' may sound a lovely idea, you may wonder what it would actually look like in practice. It requires regular effort to maintain your inspiration, keep your soul aloft and your enthusiasm fresh, and to keep on growing. Here are eight of my favourite ways of working on my business and I hope they will inform and inspire you to the ways that you can work on your business too:

1. *Read: become a voracious reader.* Have a variety of books on the go – perhaps one on personal and spiritual growth, a novel and an entrepreneurial book. Books feed, teach and inspire us; learning by reading is wonderful.

2. *Reflect and celebrate: enjoying taking a step back in order to think and feel, to wonder, integrate, be touched, inspired.* Ask lots of questions as a way of coaching yourself, such as: what has worked? What didn't work? What did I most enjoy? What didn't I enjoy? What touched me? What hurt me? How can I contribute more effectively? How could this be easier for me?

3. *Attend lectures and workshops for your continuing education.* Continually educate yourself by learning new strategies and exposing yourself to new ideas and topics.

4. *Do your 'inner work': notice where did your buttons get pushed.* Where do you have anger and resentment issues to let go of? Where are you limiting yourself? In what ways are you still being harsh and unkind to yourself?

5. *Research: enjoy looking at what others are doing, often in unrelated areas, so you can learn and be inspired by them.* Enjoy studying other people's businesses and seeing what works and what doesn't work in what they do.

6. *Go on holiday.* Have time away from home; take proper breaks so that you come back refreshed, revived and energised.

7. *Develop coaching and mentoring relationships.* In most areas of life, people receive coaching to help them perform at their best – most people don't create success in isolation. So, who can coach you? Can you create a co-coaching relationship? Is there someone who'd be willing to mentor you?

8.   *Make room for prayer, inner listening and intuitive
     guidance.* I believe that there is a greater force
     which is forever nudging us to evolve. Create the
     time and space to listen to your small, still voice of
     inner wisdom. My highest prayer is always one of
     surrender: 'Dear God (or Life or Universe), please
     use me.'

I still feel like I am in a life-long recovery programme
from the Protestant work ethic. For me, the tendency to
keep myself busy and the potential to feel guilty if I am
not busy are never far away. But I want to encourage
you as an Inspired Entrepreneur to understand the value
of working on yourself and *on* your business, as well as
working in it. It is crucial to your long-term sustainability
and to your staying in love with what you do and being
able to serve your clients in the future. As Abraham
Hicks said: 'Hard work is not the path to well-being.
Feeling good is the path to well-being. You don't create
through action; you create through vibration. And then,
your vibration calls action from you.'

In my experience, we often have patterns of thinking or
inherited beliefs which cause us to take what we love
and turn even that into hard work. Your business is both
a creative, living organism and a collection of systems.
Often people who are evolving the business they were
born to create may resist the idea of systems because
they want everything to be individual and personal.
But I don't think it is an either/or situation. You can use
systems to leverage yourself, serve more people, make
more money and have more fun.

Design a business model
that works for you

'Drive thy business or it will drive thee.'
Benjamin Franklin (1706–1790)
One of the Founding Fathers of the United States

One of the ways to work on the business you were born to create is to design and develop the business model that supports you personally. All too often I see people distorting themselves to fit their business. Sadly, it is easy to end up working *for* your business rather than have your business work for *you*.

Often when I start to talk about business models, people's eyes begin to glaze over. Perhaps this is because they don't see themselves as business people, or they believe that any mention of a business model smacks of corporate efficiency and lacks heart. Maybe twelve years ago I would have agreed with them. I had left a corporate career to escape that heartless world and ran a mile from any invitations I received to go back. Back then, I believed that a business model was something you had to bolt on to what you loved, and then you had to compromise yourself to fit into it.

Today, I think about business models quite a lot, and thoroughly enjoy doing so. Let me explain why. To me a business model is this:

• It is the way we can most effectively deliver our ideas, inspiration and experience to others, ensuring that we reach the most people.

- In the process, it helps to keep us feeling alive, inspired and passionate about what we do.
- It gives us the space for whatever else is important in our lives and enables us to create a great living.

I hope that definition excites you as much as it does me!

My interest in business models came about, as it does for most people, by my not getting things completely right. In 1997, before I had written any books, my main business income was from giving talks and workshops around the UK, and sometimes abroad. I loved doing it and was honoured to be asked to do it, and would pretty much say 'yes' to every invitation that came my way. I was happy to be doing my work, and spiritually fulfilled, but on an emotional and physical level, I was approaching burnout and not making enough money. Here is why:

- *I was running myself ragged*: I was getting tired from frequent travel.
- *I continually had to show up to earn money*: if I didn't show up, I didn't earn anything.
- *I didn't value myself very highly*: I was doing a lot of things which individually earned me small amounts of money, but not much that earned me a lot of money.
- *I had no recurring income*: no ways of earning money that didn't entail yet more work. In effect I was doing what most of us do, i.e. sell our time in return for money.

So, while on some levels I was happy because I was in demand, on another level I was tired and not enjoying it so much, and I didn't really feel that I was receiving as much as I was giving out. I identified two areas in which I wanted to take action:

1. *To release more of the hard work ethic that I had grown up with* – the belief that life was or had to be tough, even when I was doing what I loved.

2. *To create a new business model* – i.e. different and more elegant ways of earning income from doing what I loved, so that I could carry on doing it and loving it.

I developed a new motto: to be able do something once and then to be paid for it over and over again. I started doing this by 'productising' my knowledge and expertise. This allowed me to:

- Start creating multiple streams of income.
- Start creating some passive streams of income – creating opportunities to do something once and being paid for it repeatedly.
- Value myself more; charge more; say yes to higher-paying opportunities.
- Create higher-end programmes and create more income.

As I have mentioned before, my mantra today is this: there are lots of things that I love doing – writing, speaking, coaching, running workshops, mentoring, broadcasting, creating new programmes, sitting and thinking, reflecting – but none of them would I want to do every day. I love the variety, the balance, and the richness that I experience. And some days I love doing none of them!

- I love writing, but if I had to do it every day, I would get lonesome.
- I love speaking, but if I had to travel every day to give talks my nerves would become frazzled and I'd become very tired.

- I love the depth of connection that can come with one-to-one coaching, but would miss the buzz of a group if I had to work with individuals every day.
- I love being in public and meeting lots of people, but on other days I relish and savour my solitude.
- I love being with fellow soul friends, brainstorming, having conversations or simply sharing stories, yet at other times I'm happy to spend time with people from completely different walks in life for the stimulation their company can bring.

Think about what you would love your business to look like. What is your vision?

- Energy wise – what would energise you?
- Talent wise – how would you feel most positively utilised?
- Financially – what do you want and need?
- People wise – how would your work fit around your family, partner, home and community?

When you have a vision in mind, you can begin the process of creating a business that is truly going to work for you as well as for your clients.

Build a supportive community and avoid naysayers

'If we don't connect with other entrepreneurial spirits on a regular basis, our own entrepreneurial dreams are going to weaken and wither. We have to stay connected when things are going great – and when they're not.

Barbara Winter
Author of Making a Living without a Job

A crucial aspect of structuring your life as an Inspired Entrepreneur is to belong to a positive community and to limit the amount of negativity you let in. I suggest that you consciously plan how to achieve this, as you will evolve at the rate of the tribe that you're plugged into. Your journey is your own, but it can be much more fun and effective to journey alongside like-minded souls and friends, which often quickens your journey along too.

Isolation and a sense of loneliness nearly caused me to give up in my early days. I hadn't realised that it would be much easier to integrate inspiration and creativity into my life when I surrounded myself with other inspirational and passionate people.

Sadly, one of the biggest challenges you may face when you try to alter the direction of your own life is that you find yourself surrounded by people who don't want you to change. These may be people who are stuck in old ways themselves, who don't want you to follow your dreams because then they'll feel bad about not following their own; who are worried that you might fail or would rather have you stick to the conventional paths that they have trodden themselves. They may see adventure and pioneering behaviour as reckless rather than exciting.

Whilst in your early days as an Inspired Entrepreneur you probably feel a lot of inspiration, excitement and anticipation, you may well experience a lot of fear and doubt too. You could really do without adding other people's fears and doubts to those of your own, as stacking these on top of your already fragile dreams and hopes may prove to be too great a weight for you to carry.

However, you are highly likely to come across those I call the 'naysayers': people who at best feed your own doubts, and who at worst are actively hostile to you and critical of you. These are often the very people who are close to you, whom you love and who love and care for you too. Such negativity can cause a huge amount of tension and friction. To counter those influences, I suggest joining or creating a community of like-minded souls who are encouraging, supportive and not threatened by the changes you are making.

But beware: you are likely to receive a tremendous amount of unsolicited and often erroneous advice from people. Some advice may be helpful but some may not be, and it can often be hard to tell which is which. One suggestion I have is that you always consider the source of the advice. For instance, perhaps someone who has only ever had a job decides to share their opinions about self-employment with you. Does that person really have any relevant experience themselves or are they only an 'arm-chair expert?' – Perhaps they have done lots of reading on the subject but have no personal experience? There is a line from the mystic poet Rumi that has always served as a useful reminder to me: 'When embarking upon an adventure, do not consult someone who has never left home.' Ultimately, your business is there to serve you and to serve your clients – not to fit criteria imposed on it by other people, however well intentioned they may be.

Sadly, too many people end up feeling like a slave to their business rather than that their business is serving them. There are a whole series of skills involved in creating a business which truly serves you and which you can stay in love with.

Give yourself permission to define and create success for yourself

'It is because the world is so full of suffering that your happiness is a gift.'

Dr Robert Holden
Author of Success Intelligence

It sounds so obvious, but one of the most powerful things you can do for yourself is simply this: give yourself permission to succeed. That means emotional, mental, financial, material and spiritual success. In essence this boils down to giving yourself permission to be happy, freeing yourself from any guilt and fears that you may have around success. This is your lifelong journey. There is a natural happiness and success within you and you can let this out. The happier you are, the more successful you are likely to be.

This advice sounds like it should be easy to follow, but I find for many people – myself included – there are various parts of our minds, our thinking and our beliefs that go against ourselves and which are not headed in the direction of success. We don't always support ourselves, we are harsh on ourselves, and we may even be punishing ourselves. As a friend of mine once said to me, 'I don't need an enemy; I can be my own worst enemy.' There may be areas in which we feel guilty about achieving success or afraid of it. Mostly we do this unconsciously – we don't really even realise we are doing it. We all have self-undermining behaviours, the ways in which we sabotage and stop ourselves, and stories we tell ourselves about what we can't do and how we shouldn't succeed. It takes courage, skill and work to overcome them. So don't be hard on yourself for being hard on yourself. The way through is by correcting your thinking, not punishing yourself. Learn, grow and forgive yourself.

Rest assured that it is a very generous act to realise your own potential and succeed. When you do, you'll be happier – and your happiness will be a gift to everyone. As I have explained earlier, your success is a gift and a blessing for us all. In the process of realising your potential, you will have to face your fears, overcome inner demons and free yourself from limiting ideas about who you are. And as you do so you will inspire us all and give us all hope.

We are often afraid that we will fail, look stupid, lose others' love or approval, go crazy, go broke, screw up our lives or lose ourselves if we wander off a conventional career path; and these are obviously legitimate concerns. By they often act as a smoke screen to an even deeper fear that we may not even be aware of. And as Steven Pressfield expresses so eloquently in *The War of Art:* 'The Mother of all fears is so close to us that even when we verbalise it we don't believe it. The fear that we will succeed.' We fear that we will be truly happy if we listen to our inner voice, accessing those gifts and talents that our inner voice tells us we have, and becoming masterful at something we care deeply about. We fear that we do have the courage, guts and perseverance to beat our resistance and to give birth to our potential. We fear that people will actually listen to us, trust us and follow us, because then we will become visible and may be found wanting. We fear this because then many of the beliefs we grew up with and all the rules we were told to follow may turn out to be untrue.

Permission to succeed often involves giving yourself many other forms of permission, such as: the permission to take risks; to be a beginner again and not to be brilliant to start with; to be vulnerable; to ask for help; to be seen and known. Giving yourself new permissions as you go may be an important part of your journey. You may well need to give yourself permission to learn to become a successful entrepreneur after a lifetime spent as an employee.

Another piece of encouragement that I'd like to offer is this: for most of us, when we discuss success, it usually seems to be about the future, and what is going to happen. While it's wonderful to look ahead for what will be, be sure to enjoy what already is. Look out for, notice and enjoy everything that is a success now, because what you appreciate appreciates, so the more you notice the blessings you already have, the more will be given to you.

Support your longevity and your mastery

'Don't be afraid if things seem difficult in the beginning. That's only the initial impression. The important thing is not to retreat; you have to master yourself.'

Olga Korbut
Gymnast and four-time Olympic gold medallist

Success in the world may sometimes come quickly for us, but it often takes time – sometimes longer than we might expect. And even when we do find success, life goes on afterwards and there will be occasions when things don't work out so well, or there will be new thresholds of success for us to cross. It is a wise idea to temper your enthusiasm today with a longer-term vision of your goals, so that you can develop a true mastery of what you love. But this sort of long-term strategy doesn't always come easily, especially when we can see how things *could be* and want to be there already. My friend Barbara Winter says, 'The curse of the visionary is impatience.'

Twenty years ago, I attended three seminars with the US motivational speaker Tony Robbins. I came away from those seminars with a list of goals as long as my arm, but afterwards I found that I was becoming angry with myself and depressed for not achieving my goals straightaway. My desperation to succeed and over-enthusism were nearly the breaking of me. It has taken me years to learn patience and to get a handle on my desperation, and as I continue to learn these skills, success flows more easily for me. So I would advise you strongly to learn to recognise the difference between enthusiasm and over-enthusiasm.

Here are some ideas to help keep your enthusiasm alive over the long term:

1. *Do what you love*: you obviously need to love and have a passion for what you do if you are going to be doing it for another five, ten, twenty, thirty years. It must be connected in some way to your heart and soul; you need to know that you are following your own North Star and living your own authentic life.

2. *Expect few big breakthroughs, and more of an accumulation of small victories*: your success is less likely to come from a few big breakthroughs than through an accumulation of small successes and victories. Your self-esteem will grow a step at a time, as will your confidence and skill. Build your character, handle your demons and insecurities one step at a time.

3. *Be a life-long learner*: create a life of longevity by cherishing your love of both learning and unlearning. You'll need to love learning new ideas and skills, and also to be willing to relinquish the ideas that no longer serve you. Celebrate what you do know and be willing to continually learn what you don't know.

4. *Learn to deal with success, victories and triumphs, as well as loss, disappointment and failure*: during your working life there will be highs and lows, successes and failures, triumphs and defeats – and you need to learn to endure them all. Establish

a way of being in which the idea of success and
failure starts to fade, simply to be replaced by the
idea of 'experience'. Everything becomes simply an
experience. Some experiences are more pleasant
than others, but you realise they are all part and
parcel of being on your authentic path.

When we are in the business we were born to create
for the long haul, we will have to stay true to our
deeper calling, whilst at the same time putting many
incarnations of ourselves out into the world. Doing the
work we love will shape, mould and form us into what
we have always been in potential. An Estonian proverb
says, 'The work will teach you how to do it.' We shape
our work and our work shapes and teaches us. In the
process, we develop depth and wisdom.

Today, we are likely to live longer than our ancestors did,
and each decade can be an unfolding of our wisdom
and potential. Increasing numbers of people are doing
amazing things in their advanced years. My friend Dipak
ran his first marathon at the age of sixty-five; poet and
songwriter Leonard Cohen had a sell-out world tour at
seventy-four and is enjoying his greatest success; I even
read recently about a woman who did her first parachute
jump at the age of eighty-five. These days, age is less of a
barrier and more of a maturing into new capacities and
greater wisdom. We can start doing what we love at any
age, just as we can keep on doing it and succeeding at it
at any age.

Section 8:

Being an Agent
of the Infinite

Creating the business we love is a wonderful of way of serving a higher purpose. It means that we become agents of the Infinite; portals in time, using our gifts and talents to bring forth ideas from the timeless and eternal realm into the time-bound realm here on earth. We serve the gods and are supported by angels, Muses and other invisible forces. We become the servants of a greater mystery. Our job is to help humanity return a step closer home to Heaven through the work we do in our business.

You are an agent
of the Infinite

"We must offer ourselves to God like a clean, smooth canvas and not worry ourselves about what God may choose to paint on it, but at each moment, feel only the stroke of His brush."

**Jean Pierre de Caussade,
French Jesuit priest and writer**

Ultimately, through doing the work we love, we will arrive at a model of inspiration, creativity and a way of being entrepreneurial that suggests there may be higher realms of existence – of which we can prove nothing, but from which arise all ideas, all work and creativity. It is my personal belief that these realms are constantly communicating with our earthly realm. The mystic poet William Blake said, 'Eternity is in love with the creations of time', by which I think he meant that these higher realms do not merely observe us, but are active participants in our personal and collective evolution. They don't just cheer us on; they inspire us and help us to manifest our ideas in this earthly realm.

Consider this: you personally are a conduit between the eternal realm and the time-bound realm. Understood this way, you are an agent of the Infinite, here on earth to bring projects, ideas and art into existence that don't currently exist but which will exist because of you. You are the midwife, the carrier and expresser of divine ideas from higher realms into this earthly realm – and your business is simply the vehicle through which you achieve that task in this world.

In the higher realms, all ideas, businesses, art and creativity exist in potential. We become the means by which they move from formless potential into physical and time-bound actuality. As creative souls, we are the willing servants of those intentions, the servants of the great mystery. And our only enemy is our small-time ego, which generates resistance and stands guard at the door to our own gold and treasures.

So, as agents of the Infinite, we need to be warrior-like yet humble. We are not the source of the great works we bring into existence, but we facilitate their existence here. We shape and express divine ideas into this world. We are the willing and skilled instruments of whichever gods or goddesses we serve.

Marianne Williamson wrote in her book *Illuminata*: 'So it is that we all long for meaningful work, some creative endeavour that will be our ministry, by which the energies within us may flow into the world. Our activity in the world is our work. Our primary work, as we have already established, is to love and forgive. Our secondary work is our worldly employment. The meaning of work, whatever its form, is that it be used to heal the world.' We can work in an office, a practice, a hairdressing salon, a plumbing outlet, a bank, ward, classroom or boardroom – and still be an agent of the Infinite.

Any work can become your ministry. Indeed, your true job description should read 'Agent of the Infinite,' whatever your earthly job description might say. You are here to serve humanity in some unique way, to brighten the world, to help restore it to truth. And the major thing that stops you is resistance, which is why I have emphasised the idea of 'being a pro' – being professional in your work and business – so strongly earlier on in this book. When you find that you can't be an instrument of love, your job is to heal your mind of the fear and guilt within it so that you can become one.

There is a place for you and your work – you have a destiny

'Destiny is a choice consisting of knowing and understanding your soul and then making choices everyday to fulfil your soul's dreams. Ensure your daily choices are aligned with your soul's path.'

Carmen Bell,
South African entrepreneur

When you are truly living on purpose, there is a quality about you that is attractive and appealing: you are in touch with your own essence. This touches people; they will resonate with you and be drawn into your sphere. When you are working with love and from love, you will attract others. So it becomes less about what you *do*, and more about *the doing of* it as an act of love and contribution, truly desiring to uplift others. When you work with love, you are aligned to the highest vibration on earth. Truly loving what you do, and being skilful at doing it, are among the best marketing tools you have at your disposal.

For many years I've participated in running a series of seminars on creative writing and how to get a book published. One question I've heard over and over again from participants is: 'But I'm not sure I have anything new to say. Hasn't it all been said before by people more eloquent than me? Who'd want to listen to me?' I've thought about this long and hard, and my response is: 'Yes, we are all doing similar things and, yes, it has all been done and said before. But you are here to do and say it in your own authentic way, with your insights and life experience. When you are authentic and passionate about your subject, there will be people who want and like your way of doing things. Your originality comes from embracing your authenticity because you are unique and no one else does it like you do.'

I shared the same thoughts as the participants at the seminars when I started to write my first book, *The Work We Were Born To Do* – far wiser people than me had been writing about the subjects of callings and vocations for thousands of years, so what could I possibly add to it? But I wrote it anyway, drawing on my own insights and unique experience, and the book became a bestseller.

As I've mentioned before, what *won't* work for you is if you try to follow a formula and mould yourself into an image that you think will be attractive and acceptable to others, but which isn't authentically you. You will be most successful when you find out who you already are in embryo and grow that individual, rather than try to cram yourself into some idea about how you are supposed to be as an entrepreneur or person. Trying to edit and hide your authenticity will only leave you feeling dead inside, however successful you may become.

Let yourself blossom into all that you already possess within yourself. Embrace your strengths, your gifts, love and talents, and also embrace your humanity, your vulnerability, foibles and challenges. The more authentic you become, the more you will find that much of what has been your individual experience is actually universal and shared by many other people as well. You will strike a chord and create a resonance.

Working territorially for a greater good

'We might not know how or where our talents might be best put to use, but the Holy Spirit does... surrender our plans to God.'

Marianne Williamson
Author of A Return to Love

Perhaps one of the greatest transitions you can make as you move from being employed to being an Inspired Entrepreneur is a shift in orientation, from working hierarchically to working territorially. But what does that mean?

For most of our lives, the majority of us will have been trained to act hierarchically and to fit into some kind of pecking order. We need know where we stand with our teachers, parents, siblings, bosses, leaders and colleagues. We need to know how to act, what to think, feel and believe so that we will still belong to and be loved by them.

Perhaps we were once employed by our company, our boss, our team, even our country. But now, when we approach our work from a territorial perspective, our outlook will be different. Now, as well as working for money and status, we are working on behalf of something greater than ourselves: God, gods, the Universe, Heaven, Life – call it what you will.

When we work hierarchically, we work predominantly for approval, status and recognition and, of course, where the money is. As we have seen, the extreme version is a hack, someone who thinks, 'What will increase my standing? What is hot and will make me money? What will make me rich and famous?' But when we work territorially we look hard at the one place where most people don't look – inside ourselves. We ask ourselves questions such as, 'What wants to come into being through me? What I am pregnant with? What is inspiring me to take action? What can I give birth to? What am I a conduit for?'

When we work territorially, we are not originators; we are vehicles, midwives. Heaven watches over us, guiding, prompting and protecting us. We align ourselves with the mysterious forces that power the Universe, and which seek to bring new life into being and to evolve creation through us. You have probably heard artists say, 'I have no idea where my next idea will come from, or even if I will ever have another good idea.' As Inspired Entrepreneurs, as artists at what we do, we work in order to manifest that which wants to come into being through ourselves, rather than for the financial rewards our work will bring us. Paradoxically, we are likely to be well rewarded for our work. But the greatest reward of all is that we get to do the work we were born to create, and we get to know ourselves deeply and fully as we do it.

When we are on our own territory, we will feel at home within ourselves. We will be in our flow – immersed in what we were born to do. We have sovereignty over ourselves when we are on our territory. When Eric Clapton picks up his guitar, he is on his territory. When Oprah Winfrey is in a TV studio, she is on hers. When Steve Davis picks up his snooker cue and walks to the snooker table, he is on his. When Nigella Lawson steps into the kitchen she's on hers. When I fire up my computer to write, or stand in front of a group to speak, I'm on mine.

Your own territory will sustain and nourish you, not because of how it makes you look or the external rewards, but because it gives back to you what you invest in it. Your work and your territory bring you back to your own centre.

So, what is your territory? Where are you most at home within yourself? Where could it be?

Your calling is community property

'The goal of the community is to make sure that each member of the community is heard and is properly giving the gifts they have brought to this world. Without the community, the individual is left without a place where they can contribute. And so the community is that grounding place where people come and share their gifts and receive from others.'

Sobonfu E. Som,
Author of The Spirit of Intimacy

Your calling is actually community property. It is meant for you, but it also blesses, uplifts and serves others. When you are doing your work, others will benefit in ways that you may never know about. So while you don't work for the feedback you may get, know that your work will have an impact.

Ultimately, when we know that we are agents of the Infinite, on earth to bring into being what doesn't yet exist but which will exist through us, it is not our business what impact our work has. Our work comes from Heaven so let it serve Heaven. In the Hindu text, the Bhagavad Gita, Lord Krishna instructs Arjuna that we have a right to our labour, but not to the fruits of our labour. We should do our work as an offering to God:

> Give the act to me
> Purged of hope and ego
> Fix your attention on the soul
> And act and do for me

With this intention, works becomes an act of meditation and spiritual devotion. We don't always know why we are inspired to do what we do, or what impact we may have, but Heaven does have a plan, does know and sees how everything fits together.

This in not an invitation to martyrdom and suffering, but actually an opening to a rich life on many different levels. It is an invitation to contribute your gifts joyfully with a healthy detachment concerning their reception. The higher spheres of consciousness are constantly communicating with you, encouraging you to bring you ideas into physical existence from the timeless realm. As an artist, as an Inspired Entrepreneur, you serve those realms, and your only enemy is your own resistance. Your job is to become receptive, warrior-like and a skilful instrument of the gods and goddesses you serve. Indeed, *A Course in Miracles* teaches us: 'Your part is essential in God's plan for salvation.' Please play your part, and give what you've got in your heart.

You have allies and invisible support

'Just as Resistance has its seat in hell, so Creation has its home in Heaven. And it's not just a witness, but an eager and active ally.'

Steven Pressfield
Author of The War of Art

Whilst you have within you resistance that resides in your ego nature, you also have within you a force that is whispering to you to grow. It is like a sunflower seed which, given the right nutrients and conditions, is compelled to grow into a beautiful plant and flower. Flowering is the seed's destiny. I believe that you have a destiny too. And you are not alone in achieving your destiny – you needn't fulfil it through sheer effort of will alone. There are psychic forces that have the opposite goal of resistance: their purpose is to help you blossom into all that you can become. These forces go by many names: *physis* (the Ancient Greek concept of Nature), angels, Muses, *daimons*, genius. Some call it our 'deeper mind' or 'highest self'. Or love, or God. Or you might simply think of it as the creative impulse that lies coiled within the DNA of human evolution. It doesn't really matter how you imagine this force; just know that it exists and that you can utilise it. What does matter is your believing that it exists and that it is there to be called upon. The benign powers of the Universe are not just witnesses, but eager and willing forces of allegiance.

As we have seen, creative people know that they are not really the originators of their work, but the midwives of it. They are looked over by something greater than their everyday thought processes. They don't necessarily know how it works, but they know that it *does* work. They know that once they are inspired, their job is to get working and, as they commit to their work, a mysterious power begins to concentrate around them; Heaven, or whatever force they believe in, comes to their aid. Unseen forces come into play; coincidences start to occur; in time they become magnetic centres of energy.

In theory it is simple: be open to inspiration, beat your resistance and get out of your own way. Angels or Muses are already whispering inspiration to you from the eternal realms, and your job, should you choose to accept it rather than succumb to resistance, is to bring those whisperings from the eternal into the time-bound realm.

This leads to the idea of surrender: there is our own will, and then there is a Higher Will – to which we submit our own. We may sometimes fear that this Higher Will might expect us to do things we don't really want to do; and this may lead to our becoming martyrs and being joyless. Actually, the very opposite is true. Heaven sees the bigger picture and knows where your talents can best be utilised, as well as who needs your skills and how to orchestrate the bringing together of your gifts with where they are needed. I think that the highest prayer we can make, which I mentioned in Section 7 and which I would like to repeat here, is: 'Dear God, dear Universe, please use me.' Become a willing instrument.

Develop a devotion
to your work

'People think I'm disciplined. It is not discipline.
It is devotion. There is a great difference.'

Luciano Pavarotti (1935–2007)

Opera singer

Real genius is the sum of its expression: the more you immerse yourself in doing what you love, the better you will become at it. As we saw in Section 2, Paul Potts immersed himself in singing for the sheer love and joy of doing it. By the time the opportunity came for him to reveal his talent to the world, he had matured and developed it. Don't expect someone to give you a lucky break; instead, practise doing what you love – immerse yourself in it, so that when the opportunities arise you are prepared. Paradoxically, as we also saw in Section 2, the less attached you are to being paid, the more you'll do it for love anyway, and thereby increase the opportunities you have to be paid to do it.

I believe the way to give meaning to our lives is by devoting ourselves to loving others, devoting ourselves to the community around us, and devoting ourselves to creating something that gives ourselves purpose and meaning. Our devotion then becomes our work, and our work becomes our devotion.

We may need motivation and discipline, to make a conscious effort of will, to start our journey, but the more we immerse ourselves in the work we love, the more our motivation will be transformed into a kind of devotion. We will form an intimacy with our work; there will be love in our relationship with it and a sense of partnership. We will grow together. We will shape each other and develop an ever-deepening relationship with each other: our work becomes the way in which we share our love in this world.

So, now is the time to let the business you were born to create become a vehicle for something that is greater than all of us.

Conclusion

'Come now, noble souls, and take a look at the splendour you are carrying within yourselves! But if you do not let go of yourself completely, if you do not drown yourself in this bottomless sea of the Godhead, you cannot get to know this divine light.'

Meister Eckhart (c.1260–c.1327)
Medieval theologian, philosopher and mystic

A rallying call – you are here for purpose, so please give us what you've got!

You are on this planet now for a purpose, you were created for a reason and are a unique corner of creation. When you don't fulfil that purpose, you rob yourself, you rob me and you rob the world. I'm not saying this to guilt trip you, but to inspire you. Please, make visible what – without you – might perhaps never be seen. Let your work be the way your soul becomes visible in this world. Expressing your talents through the work you were born to create is not a selfish act, but actually one of the most generous things you can do. It is gift to the world and to everyone in it.

Please give yourself the gift of happiness and fulfilment: it is your destiny and in your heart to do it. Please, please show up and give us what you've got. Bless us with your gifts. You know you promised to…

Affirming Beliefs for Creating the Business You Were Born to Create

Here are some affirmations to help you on the path to the business you were born to create. You might find it helpful to write them down and place them where they will catch your eye, or to memorise one each day.

- Your existence is a blessing.

- You and your work were born into this world together.

- At the deepest level of your being, you know who you are and what you are here to be and do.

- You are significant, with incredible potential.

- You can be inspired beyond your fears to uncover the treasures in your soul.

- Your job in this lifetime is not to shape yourself into some ideal you imagine you ought to be, but to find out who you are already – and to become that person fully.

- You have a specific personal destiny – work to do, a calling to enact and a self to become.

- Your work and business are a canvas for your soul's blossoming.

- You are the steward of a unique set of gifts and talents.

- The world needs what you've got – there are people who need you to live your purpose, and you serve us all most powerfully by finding your rightful place.

- Your true creative work is a generous act and a gift to everyone.

- You can be paid for the work you work you were born to do and wrap a successful business around it.

- As an artist, you have gifts to share and need to share them generously for your own happiness.

- You know deep down, that on the other side of each of your fears lies a new freedom.

- You are seeking your own brilliance, which you can bring to your work, business and clients.

- You are an agent of the Infinite, here to bring into existence that which doesn't yet exist, but will through you.

- You are given a little corner of creation to serve, transform and set free.

- You were created to nudge humanity a step closer to Heaven with your gifts.

Join the Inspired Entrepreneur Community

'When you are in the deep end of the creative pool surrounded by others full of energy and ideas and examples, you learn to swim a lot better.'

Danny Gregory
Artist and entrepreneur

Inspirational reading:

- Nick Williams suggested reading list to support you in creating and running *The Business You Were Born To Create*. These are all books I have personally read and loved and have inspired and supported my own entrepreneurial spirit.

- Beck, Martha – *Finding Your Own North Star*

- Boldt, Laurence – *How To Find The Work You Love*

- Cameron, Julia – *The Artists Way*

- Canfield, Jack – *The Success Principles*

- Cashman, Kevin – *Leadership From the Inside Out*

- Gerber, Michael – *The E-Myth Revisited*

- Godin, Seth - *Tribes*

- Godin, Seth - *Linchpin*

- Holden, Dr Robert - *Success Intelligence*

- Holder, Jackee - *Be Your Own Best Life Coach*

- Hopson, Barrie and Ledger, Katie – *And What Do You Do?*

- Jones, Emma – *Working 5 to 9*

- Leider, Richard J – *The Power of Purpose*

- Lessor, Elizabeth - *Broken Open*

- Levoy, Gregg – *Callings*

- Matthews, Andrew – *Follow Your Heart*

- McDermott, Ian - *Boost Your Confidence With NLP*

- McCrudden, Colin, Bourne, Adrian and Lyons, Christopher – *Building a Portfolio Career*

- Palmer, Parker - *Let Your Life Speak*

- Peters, Tom – *Brand You 50*

- Pink, Daniel – *Drive*

- Pink, Daniel – *A Whole New Mind*

- Port, Michael - *Book Yourself Solid*

- Power, Penny - *Know Me, Like Me, Follow Me*

- Pressfield, Steven - *The War of Art*

- Purkiss, John and Royston-Smith, David - *Brand You*

- Secretan, Lance – Inspire – *What Great Leaders Do*

- Sharma, Robin – *The Leader Who Had No Title*

- Sharma, Robin – *The Greatness Guide*

- Sinek, Simon - *Start With Why*

- Sinetar, Marsha – *Do What You Love And The Money Will Follow*

- Spangler, David – *The Call*

- Whyte, David - *Crossing the Unknown Sea*

- Williams, Nick - *The Work You Were Born To Do*

- Williams, Nick – *How to Be Inspired*

- Williams, John - *Screw Work, Lets Play*

- Williamson, Marianne - *A Return to Love*

- Winter, Barbara - *Making A Living Without A Job*

Join the Inspired Entrepreneur Community now for £1!

Nick Williams and his business partner, Niki Hignett, love helping you reach your potential and have created the Inspired Entrepreneur Community in London, and globally too, to support you. Membership includes between one and three talks a month, gatherings, workshops, retreats and teleseminars. It will give you the inspiration, knowledge, know-how and the sense of community you need to support you and your entrepreneurial dreams.

- Premium membership costs just £12.99 per month and you can try the first month for just £1.

- Silver membership is just £4.99 a month and is for you if you can't attend the live events, enabling you access to all the downloads. Again, you can try the first month for just £1.

So if you'd like to invite Nick to speak to your group, retain him to coach or mentor you, or join the Inspired Entrepreneur Community, please contact him by any of the means below:

Nick Williams
nick@inspired-entrepreneur.com
www.inspired-entrepreneur.com
Daily Inspiration on Twitter: @nickwilliams1

Blog: www.inspired-entrepreneur.com/blog
Facebook: www.inspired-entrepreneur.com/facebook/nick

Tel. **0208 346 1551**

Nick Williams,
Heart at Work,
PO Box 2236,
London,
W1A 5UA

Nick Williams is passionate about helping people discover the work they were born to do and build successful businesses around that work. He'd love to help you.

His main services are:

- Keynote speaking

- Workshops

- Coaching and mentoring

- Broadcasting

Please contact his office direct if you would like to get Nick involved in your project.